DISCOVER
THE OCEANS

THE WORLD'S LARGEST ECOSYSTEM

— DISCOVER YOUR WORLD SERIES —
EXPLORE COOL SCIENCE | AMAZING HISTORY
16 ACTIVITIES

Lauri Berkenkamp
Illustrated by Chuck Forsman

Nomad Press is committed to preserving ancient forests and natural resources. We elected to print *Discover the Oceans: The World's Largest Ecosystem* on 3,194 lb. of Rolland Enviro100 Print instead of virgin fibres paper. This reduces an ecological footprint of:

Tree(s): 27
Solid waste: 783kg
Water: 74,033L
Suspended particles in the water: 5.0kg
Air emissions: 1,719kg
Natural gas: 112m3

It's the equivalent of:
Tree(s): 0.6 American football field(s)
Water: a shower of 3.4 day(s)
Air emissions: emissions of 0.3 car(s) per year

Nomad Press made this paper choice because our printer, Transcontinental, is a member of Green Press Initiative, a nonprofit program dedicated to supporting authors, publishers, and suppliers in their efforts to reduce their use of fiber obtained from endangered forests.

For more information, visit www.greenpressinitiative.org

Illustrations by Chuck Forsman

Questions regarding the ordering of this book should be addressed to
Independent Publishers Group
814 N. Franklin St.
Chicago, IL 60610
www.ipgbook.com

Nomad Press
2456 Christian St.
White River Junction, VT 05001

CONTENTS

OTHER TITLES IN THE *DISCOVER YOUR WORLD* SERIES

DISCOVER THE AMAZON

THE WORLD'S LARGEST RAINFOREST

DISCOVER YOUR WORLD
EXPLORE COOL SCIENCE | AMAZING HISTORY
20 ACTIVITIES

focus on **environment**

Lauri Berkenkamp
Illustrated by Blair Shedd

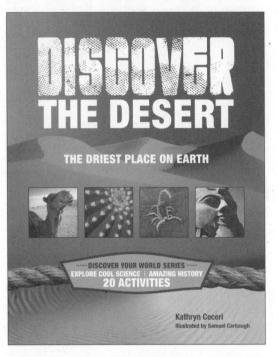

DISCOVER THE DESERT

THE DRIEST PLACE ON EARTH

DISCOVER YOUR WORLD SERIES
EXPLORE COOL SCIENCE | AMAZING HISTORY
20 ACTIVITIES

Kathryn Ceceri
Illustrated by Samuel Carbaugh

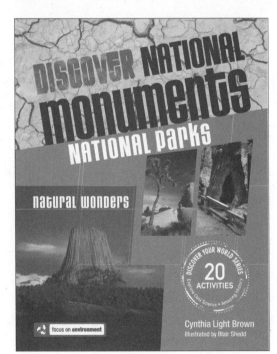

DISCOVER NATIONAL monuments NATIONAL parks

natural wonders

DISCOVER YOUR WORLD SERIES
20 ACTIVITIES
Explore Cool Science · Amazing History

focus on **environment**

Cynthia Light Brown
Illustrated by Blair Shedd

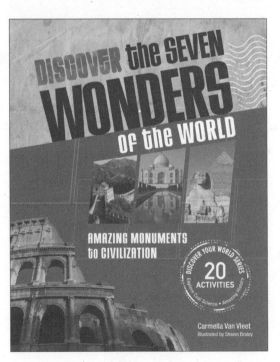

DISCOVER the SEVEN WONDERS of the WORLD

AMAZING MONUMENTS to CIVILIZATION

DISCOVER YOUR WORLD SERIES
20 ACTIVITIES
Explore Cool Science · Amazing History

Carmella Van Vleet
Illustrated by Shawn Braley

INTRODUCTION

Earth's Largest Ecosystem

The ocean is the largest **ecosystem** on the earth. It covers more than 70 percent of the earth's surface. It contains almost 99 percent of the entire living space on Earth, and almost all of the planet's water. It is home to the world's largest animal, largest volcano, deepest canyon, and highest waterfall—all under water. And yet the ocean is the least explored environment on the planet.

This book will introduce you to some of the most amazing aspects of the world's oceans. You'll learn how oceans are formed, what seawater is made of, and why ocean water is salty. You'll also learn how to navigate at sea without a compass or a map, and get to know some of the incredible creatures that live in this huge expanse of water. You'll also discover just what an extreme environment the ocean is and get to know the people and creatures who have called the ocean home for thousands of years.

Each section of this book covers a different topic. You can read the book straight through or skip around to find the information you find most interesting or useful. **What Is the Ocean?** and **Below the Surface** give you an overview of the vast expanses of water that make up the world's oceans. If you'd like to learn about how all ocean life is interconnected, turn to **The Ocean Food Web**. You'll discover that animals and plants live everywhere in the ocean—from the sunny surface to the cold, crushing depths of the deepest ocean canyons, and that they all rely on each other for survival. If you're curious about the first humans who explored the ocean and how people travel upon and underneath it, turn to **Seafaring and Ocean Exploration**. And if it's navigation you're interested in, check out **Ocean Navigators**. You'll be introduced to some of the ways ocean-going people have navigated for centuries. You'll also learn about ocean currents, how to read wave patterns, and how to set a course using the sun, moon, stars, and ocean itself. If you'd like to learn a little more about how to cope with the extreme ocean environment, turn to **Surviving Ocean Extremes**, where you'll learn how to avoid seagoing dangers like sunburn, dehydration, and hypothermia.

Throughout the book you'll find fascinating facts and sidebars that look closely at some of the most incredible plants, animals, and people of the oceans, from the tiny **copepod** to the great white shark. You'll also find *Try This* activities that you can do anywhere—you don't have to be on the ocean—ranging from learning how to make a solar still or a simple fishing spear to experimenting with a home-made diving bell or figuring out how much water you really need to stay alive.

Oceans cover a vast portion of our planet and have a huge influence on all of our lives—and the life of every living thing. It will take our knowledge and combined efforts to keep the world's waters healthy and thriving. Ready to jump into the salty spray and discover the oceans? Let's get going!

WORDS TO KNOW

ecosystem: a community of plants and animals living in the same area and relying on each other to survive.

copepod: a tiny animal related to shrimp.

CHAPTER 1

What Is the Ocean?

 Our planet is covered in water. The oceans cover more than two-thirds of the earth's surface and contain almost all of the living space on the planet. That's because the living space of the oceans is both on and below the surface. Miles below the surface.

The oceans have many different names—Pacific, Atlantic, Indian, Arctic, and Southern. But they are really part of one enormous water system that flows all over the globe. Water from the frigid Arctic Ocean makes its way around the world to Australia. The same water that laps the rocky coast of Maine will eventually reach the beaches in Thailand. In fact, **oceanographers** call Earth's seawater a "world ocean," since all of those bodies of water are connected.

WORDS TO KNOW

oceanographer: a scientist who studies the ocean.

 3

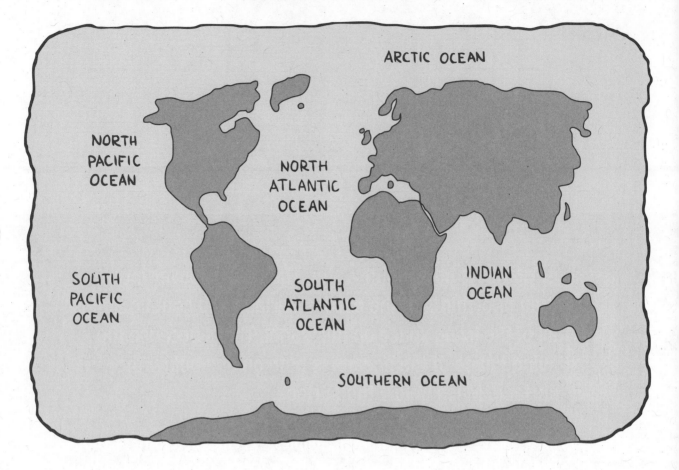

People talk about how big our oceans are. After all, Earth is known as the "blue planet" because oceans cover so much of the earth's surface that from space they make our planet look bright blue. But it can be hard to really grasp just how enormous and important the oceans are to us. Here are some facts about the world's oceans that might surprise you:

- The oceans contain 97 percent of all the water on Earth. That's about 1.4 billion trillion tons of water! If all the water in the world fit into a 2-liter soda bottle, the salt water from the oceans would fill the bottle up to the neck. Only the last 3 tablespoons would be freshwater.
- There is so much water in our oceans that if the earth were as smooth as a marble, and all the water of the world's oceans evenly covered its surface, the planet would be completely covered in a layer of water 2.25 miles (3.7 kilometers) deep.

- The oceans cover the largest mountain range, the highest waterfall, and the deepest canyon in the world. None of these can be seen by humans because they are so deep underwater!
- The Pacific Ocean alone contains half of all the world's water.
- The top 10 feet of the world's oceans hold as much heat as our entire **atmosphere**.
- Oceans cover 80 percent of the **Southern Hemisphere**, and about 40 percent of the **Northern Hemisphere**.
- The oceans control the world's **climate**, weather systems, and air temperatures.

What's the Difference Between an Ocean and a Sea?

If you look on a map, there are a lot of large bodies of water that are called seas, like the Mediterranean Sea, the Arabian Sea, and the Caribbean Sea. What's the difference between a sea and an ocean?

Seas are actually parts of oceans that are mostly surrounded by land. The Mediterranean and Caribbean Seas, for example, both connect to the Atlantic Ocean. The Arabian Sea connects to the Indian Ocean. Some seas are connected to the oceans only through other seas. The Black Sea, for example, which is almost completely **landlocked**, connects to the Atlantic Ocean through the Adriatic Sea and the Mediterranean Sea. But there are bodies of water called seas that aren't really seas at all. The biggest of these is the Caspian Sea, which is located in Asia. It is full of salt water but isn't connected to any ocean.

WORDS TO KNOW

atmosphere: the layer of air surrounding the earth.

Southern Hemisphere: the bottom half of the globe, south of the equator.

Northern Hemisphere: the half of the globe, north of the equator.

equator: the imaginary line around the earth, midway between the North and South Poles.

climate: the prevailing weather conditions of a region—temperature, air pressure, humidity, precipitation, sunshine, cloudiness, and winds—throughout the year, averaged over a series of years.

landlocked: completely surrounded by land.

WORDS TO KNOW

species: a group of living things that are closely related and physically similar.

canyon: a deep trench in the earth, often with steep sides.

Mariana Trench: the deepest part of the world's oceans, located in the Pacific, near Guam.

continental plates: the different portions of the earth's crust that move over a long time.

polyps: small creatures that live in colonies and form coral.

algae: an organism that is similar to a plant because it turns light into energy but that does not have leaves or roots.

bleaching: when coral dies, it loses its color and becomes white, or bleached.

BRANCHING OUT: THE DIFFERENT OCEANS

Even though all the seawater in the world is one giant ocean with lots of different branches, these branches aren't all the same. They are different sizes and shapes. The branches even have different characteristics and different **species** of plants and animals.

The five largest bodies (or branches) of seawater are the Pacific, Atlantic, Indian, Arctic, and Southern oceans, and all have special features that make them unique.

The Pacific Ocean is the largest ocean in the world. It covers more than a third of the entire planet, and reaches from the far north of the Northern Hemisphere to the far south of the Southern Hemisphere. The Pacific Ocean is so big that all the continents and almost all of the other oceans could fit into it.

It is also the deepest ocean, with an average depth of 13,741 feet (4,188 meters). That's more than 2½ miles (4 kilometers) deep. The deepest **canyon** in the world, called the Challenger Deep, is part of a larger canyon called the **Mariana Trench**. This canyon extends into the earth about 7 miles (11 kilometers).

Underneath the Pacific Ocean is where Earth is most active—the **continental plates** grind against each other, causing major earthquakes to occur and volcanoes to erupt.

FASCINATING FACT

The Pacific Ocean is shrinking and the Atlantic Ocean is expanding because the world's continents slowly drift each year.

In fact, there is an area in the South Pacific the size of New York State that has 1,133 active volcanoes that erupt regularly. There is at least one volcano erupting at any given time!

The Pacific Ocean isn't just the deepest and largest ocean. It is also home to one of the world's most amazing natural wonders: the Great Barrier Reef. Located off of the northeastern coast of Australia, the Great Barrier Reef is 210 separate coral reefs that stretch for more than 1,260 miles (2,028 kilometers) around northern Australia. The Great Barrier Reef is full of some of the most amazing, beautiful, and deadly sea creatures on the planet, including the Irukandji jellyfish and the great white shark.

Coral reefs are made of the hard outer skeletons of tiny animals called **polyps**, which are related to jellyfish and sea anemones. When polyps die, new polyps grow skeletons over the old. That's how coral reefs grow, but it takes a very long time. In fact, it takes about 20 years for a colony of coral to grow to be about the size of a basketball. Scientists estimate that the Great Barrier Reef began to grow about 18 million years ago and is still growing today.

Like all coral reefs, the Great Barrier Reef is affected by pollution and climate change. Coral can only grow in warm, shallow water, because most polyps eat **algae**. If water levels get too deep, the coral can't grow because there isn't enough sunlight for algae to survive. Polyps are also affected by temperature. If the temperature of the water gets too warm, the polyps die. Since the living polyps are what give coral reefs their color, when polyps die the coral reef **bleaches**. The Great Barrier Reef has been a national marine park since 1983, and the Australian government works hard to keep the reef healthy.

Great Barrier Reef

The Atlantic Ocean is the second-largest ocean in the world, about half the size of the Pacific. It is shaped like an "S" and separates Europe and Africa from North and South America. The Atlantic Ocean is home to the world's longest mountain range, called the Mid-Atlantic Ridge, which stretches 10,000 miles (16,000 kilometers) under the ocean from Iceland all the way to the southern tip of Africa.

The Atlantic Ocean is full of life, with some of the most diverse ocean plants and animals in the world. In fact, the Atlantic Ocean has the world's largest fisheries. In the spring, the sun's heat causes water temperatures to rise, and enormous **plankton** blooms create the beginning of huge **food chains**. For centuries, fishermen have sailed the Atlantic Ocean fishing grounds, using nets to pull up millions of tons of fish each year.

The Atlantic is the world's youngest ocean, and it is also the most studied—scientists know more about the Atlantic Ocean than any other. One major discovery scientists made about the Atlantic is that underneath the surface of its waters lies the world's largest waterfall. Most people think that Angel Falls, an amazing waterfall in Venezuela that drops 2,648 feet (807 meters), is the world's tallest waterfall. Think again. Deep below the surface of the Atlantic, off the coast of Denmark, is a waterfall that drops an amazing 2.2 miles (3.5 kilometers), completely underwater. That's three times as tall as Angel Falls! The water slowly cascades off an underwater cliff beneath the Denmark Straits, falling to the deep ocean floor.

The Indian Ocean is located mostly in the Southern Hemisphere, between Africa, southern Asia, Australia, and Antarctica. It's the third-largest ocean, and holds about 20 percent of the world's ocean waters.

What Is the Ocean?

Two of Asia's biggest rivers, the Indus and the Ganges, run into the Indian Ocean. Rivers carry **sediment**. So the Indian Ocean has the largest amount of river sediment in the world—underneath the waves are two enormous fans of sediment more than 1,240 miles (2,000 kilometers) wide. One of the most unusual aspects of the Indian Ocean is that its **currents** change direction with the seasons. In the winter, **monsoon** winds push currents toward Africa. Summer winds push currents toward Asia. All other oceans have currents that stay the same.

⎯FASCINATING FACT⎯

The Antarctic circumpolar current flows clockwise around Antarctica and carries more water than any other ocean current. It could fill all the Great Lakes in just two days.

Ocean Serengetis

Scientists have recently discovered areas in the ocean that are so full of wildlife that they are like the ocean version of the watering holes of the Serengeti Plains in Africa. These ocean "hotspots" are usually in convergence zones, where **tropical** and **temperate** oceans meet. They also usually have reefs or underwater **sea mounts** where lots of plankton and small fish thrive. Those smaller fish attract the major **predators**, such as tuna, swordfish, shark, and billfish. Many of these large predator fish are endangered species. The scientists who have discovered these hotspots want to turn them into protected parks, similar to national parks on land, where the fish would be protected from overfishing.

In January 2008, the island nation of Kiribati (pronounced Kir-a-bos) established the world's largest marine protected area in the Pacific Ocean. About the size of California, the ocean marine park is home to coral reefs, huge populations of fish and other sea life, and even an underwater mountain range. When scientists did a research survey of the diversity of life in the waters of Kiribati, they found more than 120 species of coral, 520 different species of fish, sea turtles, and some of the largest groups of nesting seabirds in the Pacific.

WORDS TO KNOW

plankton: microscopic plants and animals that float or drift in great numbers in bodies of water.

food chain: a community of animals and plants where each different plant or animal is eaten by another plant or animal higher up in the chain.

sediment: dirt, fertilizer, rocks, and other pieces of matter deposited in a river and in the ocean.

current: a steady flow of water in a certain direction.

monsoon: the rainy season. A time of year when it rains frequently in a certain part of the world.

tropical: the climate in the tropics, the region north and south of the equator.

temperate: the climate in the temperate zone, the regions north and south of the tropics.

sea mount: a mountain rising above the sea floor.

predator: an animal that lives by preying on, or eating, other animals.

— FASCINATING FACT —

Scientists weren't sure if there was a continent under the Arctic ice cap until 1958, when a **submarine** called the USS *Nautilus* traveled underneath the ice and discovered that there was nothing but water underneath.

The Southern Ocean surrounds the continent of Antarctica. The Southern Ocean wasn't an "official" ocean until 2000. Until then, it was usually called the Antarctic Ocean, and was considered a polar region of the other three major oceans. But scientists realized that the winds that blow around the continent of Antarctica are so strong that the surface currents of the Southern Ocean qualify it as its own ocean. The Southern Ocean's official boundaries are all the waters that lie south of 60 **degrees** south **latitude**.

The Southern Ocean is about twice the size of the United States, but it is much smaller than the other three major oceans. It is the coldest ocean on the planet, with average temperatures

WORDS TO KNOW

degree: a unit of measurement that tells people where they are on the planet.

latitude: an imaginary line that goes around the earth and runs parallel to the equator. It measures your position on earth north or south of the equator.

submarine: a type of ship that travels beneath the water rather than above it and that can stay underwater for a long time.

sea ice: ocean water that freezes.

polar ice cap: giant sheets of sea ice that float on the Arctic and Antarctic Oceans.

ranging from 28 to 50 degrees Fahrenheit (-2 to 10 degrees Celsius). In winter, more than half of the ocean is covered with ice and icebergs. The Southern Ocean is known for its extreme weather. Because there is no land to block the wind and waves that circle the globe at the southern tip, the winds can reach above 190 miles (306 kilometers) per hour.

Even though the Southern Ocean is cold, it is still full of life. In the spring, blooms of plankton form in the water. Plankton attract krill, which are tiny shrimp-like sea creatures about 1¼ inches (4 centimeters) long. Krill are the favorite food of many ocean creatures, from fish to giant whales. Giant swarms of krill look like huge red patches on the surface of the ocean. They are the first link in a huge food chain that includes fish, seabirds, seals, penguins, and whales.

The Arctic Ocean is the smallest and shallowest ocean in the world. It is also almost completely landlocked—surrounded by North America, Europe, and northern Asia. The Arctic Ocean is full of ice, and in winter, nearly the entire ocean is frozen. Because it is so hard for ships to get through the ice, even in summer, the Arctic Ocean is the least studied of all of the oceans.

Sea ice is what makes up the **polar ice caps**. Parts of the ice cap freeze and melt with the seasons, and parts of the ice cap are so thick that they stay frozen year-round. Scientists are concerned because the polar ice caps in the Arctic are getting smaller each year—ice is melting faster than new ice can be formed. Why is this a problem?

— FASCINATING FACT —

The Antarctic circumpolar current carries all of the very cold water from the Antarctic up and out to the deep ocean basins of the Atlantic, Pacific, and Indian Oceans.

First, the polar ice caps in the Arctic and Antarctica contain almost all the freshwater on the planet. If that ice melts and disappears into the ocean, most of the world's freshwater supply will disappear. Also, if the ice caps melt, the ocean water level could rise as much as 246 feet (75 meters). That would change the face of the planet, and low-lying areas would be completely covered by the ocean. For example, many island nations are only a few feet about sea level. If the oceans were to rise even 10 feet (3 meters) higher than they are today, countries such as Tuvalu, the Maldive Islands, and Kiribati would disappear.

Finally, and maybe most importantly, the ice caps act like giant mirrors. They reflect a lot of the sun's heat back into space, keeping the planet cool. As the ice caps get smaller, they can't reflect as much of the sun's energy, so the planet can't stay as cool. If the planet can't stay cool, that makes the ice caps melt faster—so it's a dangerous cycle.

WORDS TO KNOW

erosion: the process through which the earth is broken down and washed away by wind and water.

THE OCEAN IS REALLY SALTY

If you've ever swum in the ocean, you've probably tasted a mouthful of seawater. It's pretty salty. In fact, it's 220 times more salty than freshwater. That's a lot of salt! And scientists have wondered for a long time why the oceans contain so much salt. After all, freshwater pours into the oceans from rivers all over the world 365 days each year, and millions of gallons of water fall on the oceans as rain all the time. But that's actually part of the reason why the sea got so salty in the first place, and stays salty now.

All the water that hits the earth, either in the form of rain hitting the ground or running over river beds, causes **erosion**, which brings lots of

— FASCINATING FACT —

If you could take all the salt out of all of the world's oceans and spread it on land, it would cover the entire earth with a solid layer of salt more than 500 feet (152 meters) thick. That's about as tall as a 40-story office building.

minerals into the oceans, including salt. When the sun's heat causes seawater to evaporate, the salt and minerals in the oceans are left behind.

Another reason that the oceans contain a lot of salt is because of the way the earth is always changing. When oceanographers discovered superhot deep-sea vents, they learned that ocean water cycles through the earth's crust. The water flows through cracks in the sea floor until it hits very, very hot rock. The water gets superheated and dissolves minerals from the rock, then shoots back up to the surface of the seafloor through thermal vents. The minerals that dissolve into the water contain lots of salt.

So the combination of new salt being brought into the oceans and water being removed through evaporation means that the salt stays behind even when water leaves. In fact, over time—long, long periods of time—the oceans have become saltier.

TRY THIS: JUST HOW SALTY IS THE OCEAN?

You'd be surprised at how sensitive you are to salt—and just how much salt the ocean has. Fill three cups with water from your faucet. Leave one alone. Add a pinch of salt to the second one. Add a teaspoon of salt to the third one. Taste the first cup: this is freshwater, and even though there are dissolved salts and minerals in the water, there is too little for you to taste. Try the second cup: you may or may not be able to taste the salt in this, depending on your taste buds and how much you think of as a "pinch" of salt. This is called brackish water and is similar to the salt content of water in places where freshwater rivers flow into oceans. Now taste the third glass: it will taste really salty. This is about the same salt content as a glass of sea water.

Making Freshwater from Seawater

Most of the water in the world is salty—only 3 percent of all the water on Earth is freshwater. But all of the people in the world need freshwater to drink. People who live in countries where there is little or no freshwater but have easy access to seawater have turned to the ocean as a source of drinking water. They create freshwater from saltwater through a process called **desalination**. This is a process that takes the salt out of seawater and leaves freshwater behind. There are a few ways to desalinate water. One way is to boil seawater so the water **molecules** separate from the salt molecules and other minerals and turn to steam. The steam is captured and then condenses as freshwater, and the salt molecules and other minerals are left over. This is a very expensive method because it takes a lot of energy to boil off all that seawater.

Another way to desalinate seawater is through reverse **osmosis**. Seawater is pumped into a tube at high pressure through a very, very fine filter that allows water molecules to pass through but stops the salt molecules. Reverse osmosis is also expensive. It takes a lot of energy to create enough pressure to keep the freshwater that has been filtered through the membranes from moving back to dilute the salt water.

A new technology called forward osmosis might help poorer countries lower the cost of desalinating seawater in the future. Forward osmosis works a little bit like reverse osmosis: seawater is pushed through a very fine filter so the salt stays behind. But unlike reverse osmosis, where the freshwater needs to be under constant pressure so it won't filter back through the membrane to join up with the salt molecules, forward osmosis sends the freshwater into a tube containing ammonia and carbon dioxide. The freshwater molecules are attracted to the ammonia and carbon dioxide, so they keep moving in one direction, away from the salt molecules. The solution is heated, and the ammonia and carbon dioxide evaporate and are collected for reuse. What's left is freshwater. All this requires a lot less energy than reverse osmosis or boiling desalination. Researchers are experimenting with ways to perfect the process for use in the future.

WORDS TO KNOW

desalination: the process of removing salt from water.

molecules: the simplest part of an element (like oxygen) or a compound (like water).

osmosis: the process of moving water through a filter that can make it good for drinking.

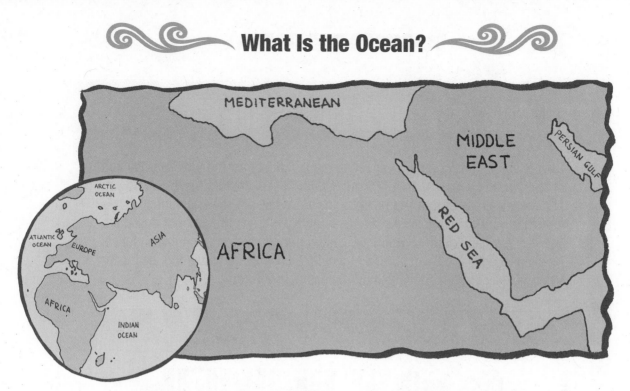

WHAT'S ACTUALLY IN SEAWATER?

Scientists have been studying the chemical makeup of seawater for almost 100 years, and they still aren't totally sure what it's made of. They have identified at least 72 chemical elements in seawater, and they are pretty sure that all of the elements that occur naturally on Earth are in the oceans, but they haven't proven it yet. One major component, obviously, is salt. But that salt content is different depending on where you are in the oceans. The warmer the water and the hotter the climate, the saltier the water will be. That's because warm water and a hot climate lead to quicker evaporation of water.

The saltiest water is in the **Red Sea** and the **Persian Gulf.** These two places are very hot, and the water evaporates very quickly. That leaves a lot of salt behind. The least salty places in the oceans are at the mouths of big rivers, near the coasts, and in the polar regions. In all of these places, a lot of freshwater mixes with salt water to make the ocean water less salty. In polar seas, the water is much less salty. That's because they contain lots of melting ice and usually a lot of precipitation, which dilutes the salt.

Red Sea: a sea located between Africa and Saudi Arabia.

Persian Gulf: a part of the Indian Ocean, located in the Middle East.

TRY THIS: HOW MUCH SALT DO YOU EAT IN A DAY?

Dietary guidelines for Americans recommend that adults and kids over the age of two take in no more than 2,400 mg (milligrams) of sodium (that's salt to you and me) a day. While that seems like a lot, you'd be surprised how much salt is hidden in your food and drinks. For one day, try to track the amount of sodium you eat. You can find the amount of sodium per serving on the nutrition labels of any packaged food, from bread and milk to cookies or soda pop. See if your average daily sodium intake is more or less than 2,400 mg.

SEA ANIMALS AND SEAWATER

You might not believe it, but fish living in salt water have to actually drink sea-water to stay alive. Why? Because their bodies have less salt than the water around them. The freshwater in their bodies is always moving toward the salt water surrounding them, so these fish have to drink all the time. They deal with all the salt they take in by pushing it out through their gills. Birds and mammals that live in the ocean have to find ways to get enough freshwater to drink, since they can't survive on seawater. Scientists aren't quite sure how some sea mammals, especially whales, get enough freshwater to keep their bodies working properly. They haven't been able to study them that closely.

But scientists have studied other mammals, especially seals and sea lions, and they think that most sea mammals get almost all of their freshwater through the foods they eat. Most sea mammals are carnivores, which means they eat meat. Animals that eat fish, such as

FASCINATING FACT

The word *ocean* comes from Okeanos, the Greek god of sea and water.

16

sea lions, get enough water from the fish they eat to survive without drinking freshwater at all. Dolphins seem to get enough water from the fish they eat and from turning fat into energy—one of the byproducts of burning fat inside your body is water.

Other mammals that eat sea plants or shellfish, such as otters, take in the same amount of salt that they would if they were actually drinking the water. These mammals have kidneys that can handle drinking seawater or eating foods that contain high amounts of salt.

Many sea mammals like to drink freshwater if they can. Seals will often eat snow to get freshwater, and manatees will swim up Florida's waterways to drink out of people's garden hoses that have been left running. Like seals, manatees don't drink seawater.

— **FASCINATING FACT** —

Manatees and their cousins, dugongs, are the only sea mammals that are vegetarians.

Some sea creatures have an even more interesting way of keeping hydrated at sea. Sea birds and sea turtles have a special adaptation that makes it okay for them to drink salty water. They have glands around their eyes, called salt (or saline) glands, that actually take the salt right out of the seawater so the water that goes through their organs is fresh. Turtles get rid of excess salt by crying salt tears. Seabirds get rid of excess salt by sneezing. Sea snakes have a saline gland under their tongues to get rid of salt, but some species of sea snakes still need to drink freshwater to survive. These snakes live near coastlines so they can leave the ocean, lay eggs, and find freshwater to drink.

CHAPTER 2

Below the Surface

Oceanographers usually divide ocean waters into separate layers, called zones, from the surface all the way to the **seafloor**. Zones are based on the amount of sunlight that can penetrate the water's layers and have appropriate names: the sunlight zone, the twilight zone, and the midnight zone. We know most about the upper layers of the ocean, because that's where humans are most able to explore. Those layers are also where most sea life can be found.

The Ocean's Layers

The Sunlight Zone is also called the euphotic zone. *Euphotic* means "good light." This is the top layer of the ocean. The sunlight zone stretches from the surface of the water to a depth of about 656 feet (200 meters). It is called the sunlight zone because it is the layer that gets the most sunlight, and it has by far the most sea life. The sunlight zone is also the warmest zone of the ocean, since it is heated by

the sun. Life in this zone ranges from the tiniest **phytoplankton**, which are microscopic plants, to the enormous whale shark, the biggest fish in the oceans.

SUNLIGHT ZONE

TWILIGHT ZONE

MIDNIGHT OR BATHYPELAGIC ZONE

ABYSSALPELAGIC ZONE

HADALPELAGIC ZONE

The top layer of the ocean is the narrowest layer, but it is the most crowded with life. Why? Because most life in the ocean begins with plants, and plants need the sun to live. Millions of species of plants, animals, and fish live in the sunlight zone. Some species can live in many different environments within this zone. Large fish, like sharks, can live near shallow reefs or hunt in the open ocean. Whales migrate for thousands of miles each year between nesting grounds and feeding grounds where they spend the rest of the year. Then there are some species of fish that will spend their entire lives within a few feet of where they were born.

Life in the sunlight zone is dangerous—lots of life also means lots of predators. Many fish and other sea creatures in the sunlight zone have a special **adaptation** called countershading to trick predators. They are darker on top of their bodies and lighter underneath. When predators are above them, the fish blend in with the darker water below. When predators are below them, the fish blend in with the lighter water above. Pretty tricky!

The Twilight Zone is the layer underneath the sunlight zone. This layer is also called the dysphotic zone. *Dysphotic* means "deficient light." Sunlight doesn't reach very deeply into this zone, which is at a depth of between 656 and 3,281 feet (200 to 1,000 meters).

WORDS TO KNOW

seafloor: the bottom of the sea or ocean.

sunlight zone: the top layer of the ocean.

phytoplankton: a type of plankton that gets its energy from the sun through photosynthesis.

adaptation: changes an animal or plant makes (or has made) in response to its environment.

twilight zone: the layer below the sunlight zone that has no light at its bottom.

The Thermocline

The thermocline is a layer of water in the twilight zone of the ocean where the water temperature drops really quickly. The sun's light and warmth keep the sunlight zone pretty warm, and the wind and waves mix that warmth to a certain depth, around 330 feet (100 meters). But below the sunlight zone the water temperature starts dropping quickly. The temperature difference from the top of the thermocline to the bottom can be as great as almost 60 degrees Fahrenheit (about 20 degrees Celsius). Below about 1,000 feet (300 meters), the ocean temperatures stay pretty much the same.

It is brightest at the top of the zone and almost completely black at the deepest point. The twilight zone is the ocean layer with the biggest difference in temperature, which can change as much as 60 degrees Fahrenheit (15 degrees Celsius) from the top of the zone to the bottom.

Food is scarce in the twilight zone because not enough light penetrates this zone for plants to grow. Creatures that live here are in stiff competition for survival, and have to have very powerful senses to stay alive and to hunt for food. Animals in the twilight zone have adapted so that they are not easily seen by predators and can capture whatever food comes their way.

Creatures in the twilight zone have really good eyesight—most of them have eyes that are very big for the size of their body, and many have adapted so that their eyes are on the top of their heads. That way they can see the shape of creatures above them reflected against the light of the higher zone.

FASCINATING FACT

The migration of creatures from the twilight zone to the sunlight zone each night to hunt is the largest migration of animals on Earth—and it happens every night!

Many animals in the twilight zone are transparent so that their predators look right through them rather than at them. Others are silvery so they blend in better with the dim light. But the most interesting adaptation of animals in the twilight zone is **bioluminescence**. Animals that are bioluminescent can make their own light. They use their bioluminescence to lure smaller prey toward them, and to confuse predators who want to eat them. It is a pretty effective adaptation, and more than 90 percent of the animals that live in the twilight zone are bioluminescent in some way.

Twilight zone animals that aren't bioluminescent have other ways to trick predators. Some have strange body shapes. Hatchet fish are completely flat, so they seem to disappear when predators look at them head-on. These fish are also covered in reflective silver scales that act like mirrors, bouncing back any light that might hit them. Other animals can change their shape, so they confuse predators. For example, when pout eels are threatened, they put their tails in their mouths and float motionless in the water. This makes them look like jellyfish, so other fish avoid eating them.

Because very little food sinks down from the sunlight zone to the twilight zone, lots of creatures who live in the twilight zone will move up to the sunlight zone to hunt at night. Just how many? Millions. So many millions, in fact, that when sailors were trying to use **sonar** at night to map the ocean bottom in the 1950s, they kept getting false bottom readings. They finally figured out that the false bottom they were measuring was a layer of millions of fish, jellyfish, squid, and other deep-water creatures that travel up to the shallower layers of the ocean to find food.

The Midnight Zone is the part of the ocean where more than 75 percent of all the ocean's water lies. It starts at 3,281 feet below the surface and goes all the way to a depth of 13,124 feet (1,000–4,000 meters). That's almost 3 miles! *Aphotic* means "no light," and this part of the ocean is called the aphotic zone because absolutely no natural light reaches this deep. It's also referred to as the **bathypelagic zone**—*bathy* means "deep water."

WORDS TO KNOW

bioluminescence: the ability to create light from a chemical reaction inside an organism's body.

sonar: an instrument that locates objects with sound waves.

midnight zone: the part of the ocean with no light.

bathypelagic zone: the zone of the ocean that is at a depth of between 3,281 and 13,124 feet.

How Does Bioluminescence Work?

In the deep ocean, where it's dark, sea creatures have adapted to make light from chemicals in their own bodies. *Bioluminescence* literally means "living light." You've probably seen a firefly flashing off and on during hot summer nights. Fireflies use bioluminescence to attract mates. You may also have used a glow stick at night—you crack the glow stick to mix a couple of chemicals and all of a sudden it starts to glow. The same thing happens to deep-sea fish. They have chemicals in their bodies that mix to make their bodies give off light. Most deep-sea creatures give off a blue-green light, because blue-green light travels farthest in the ocean, but some animals can create yellow, green, and even red light.

WORDS TO KNOW

abyssopelagic zone: the zone of the ocean that stretches from a depth of 13,124 to 19,686 feet.

ocean floor: the very bottom of the ocean.

hadalpelagic zone: the trench zone of the ocean, from a depth of 19,686 feet going all the way to the bottom of the ocean.

pressure: the amount of force that pushes upon any object.

The Abyssopelagic Zone is deeper than that, from 13,124 to 19,686 feet (4,000–6,000 meters). Its name means "bottomless," but this layer really is where most of the **ocean's floor** sits. This zone is often known simply as "the abyss" or abyssal plain, since so much of the ocean floor is wide and almost completely flat.

The Hadalpelagic Zone is the absolute deepest part of the ocean. *Hadal* means "unseen," and this zone is where the world's deep ocean trenches lie. This layer goes from a depth of 19,686 feet to at least 35,987 feet (6,000–11,000 meters). This is the depth of the Challenger Deep, which is the deepest part of the ocean ever measured. The trench is so deep that you could easily fit Mt. Everest plus a smaller mountain inside it.

In the midnight zone, the **pressure** of the water is absolutely enormous—so much that if you could go down there, it would feel like 50 jumbo jets were sitting on top of you. Creatures that live in the midnight zone are mostly made of water, because water can't be compressed by all that pressure. Since not much food (called "marine snow") drifts down this deep from the surface and the surface waters are just too far away for these fish to migrate to every night for food, these creatures have to be ready to eat anything that comes by, no matter what its size.

Creatures that live in the midnight zone have some pretty amazing adaptations to help them be success-ful hunters. They are usually black or red in color, so they are completely invisible in the inky darkness. Surprisingly, fish in the midnight zone are pretty bad swimmers. Most don't have **swim bladders** to help them stay buoyant. Also, since they don't have strong muscles they are very slow moving. So instead of chasing their prey, these dark-zone fish hunt by stealth. Most have huge jaws and very large teeth compared to the rest of their bodies so they can swallow **prey** much larger than themselves.

Since there is no natural light in the midnight zone, fish in this zone have very poor eyesight. Some don't have eyes at all! Instead, deep-sea fish are really sensitive to vibrations in the water. Most have special **cells** along the sides of their bodies that can pick up the slightest vibrations in the water. The fish keep their bodies very still and wait to feel where vibrations come from, then get ready to pounce when their prey swims by.

WORDS TO KNOW

swim bladder: an air-filled sac in many fish that helps them float.

prey: an animal that is hunted or caught for food.

cell: the most basic unit of all organisms. Billions of cells make up an animal or plant.

OCEAN VENTS AND COLD SEEPS

In 1977, a team of scientists using ROVs (remotely operated vehicles) were under the Galapagos Islands off the coast of South America and discovered superhot springs and heat vents on the ocean floor, miles below the surface. Those hot springs and vents were brimming with life. Giant tube worms survived and thrived in and around these deep-sea vents, which spewed toxic chemicals into water where absolutely no sunlight ever reached. Enormous mollusks and clams, strange pink fish, and hundreds of white crabs lived around the base of the worms. The scientists realized that the tube worms in the heat vents ate bacteria that converted the poisonous chemicals from the vents into food in a process called

chemosynthesis. Until scientists found these deep-ocean tube worms, they assumed that all life on Earth was based on **photosynthesis**, using the energy of sunlight. Following this discovery, a new species was identified in the **ecosystem** of the deep-sea vents about every 10 days.

Scientists found another new deepwater ecosystem in 1984: cold seeps. Using sonar to look at the ocean floor in the Gulf of Mexico, scientists found a weird place that looked like a lake surrounded by golden sand. The water in the lake was four times as salty as regular seawater, and full of **methane**, a natural gas. The sand was really millions of mussels that were living off the chemicals seeping from the lake. Scientists also found **ice worms**, tube worms, and even fish that lived in this very strange ecosystem.

Scientists are really excited about the heat vents and cold seeps in the midnight zone. If life can exist under the oceans where there is absolutely no sunlight and creatures can make energy from chemicals, then perhaps life can also exist on other planets with some of the same chemical combinations!

WORDS TO KNOW

chemosynthesis: a process through which organisms get energy from carbon dioxide and water instead of sun.

photosynthesis: the process through which organisms get energy from the sun.

ecosystem: a community of plants and animals living in the same area and relying on each other to survive.

methane: a colorless, odorless gas that we use as a fuel.

ice worms: a species of worm that are found living in ice.

Tube Worms

SHARKS

The most famous—and misunderstood—animals in the ocean are sharks. They certainly are the most terrifying sea creatures. The reality is that most sharks have absolutely no interest in humans at all—and most are not dangerous to humans. But it would still be scary if you were in a raft and a shark bumped you, or if you saw a triangular fin cutting through the water. Shipwreck survivors often see sharks around their rafts, but it's not because the sharks are waiting to attack them. Usually it's because rafts attract other fish. Especially in warm waters, a raft offers a nice, shady spot for fish to hang out. Those fish attract sharks.

Mini Monsters of the Deep

While all of the deep-sea fish look a little weird, one of the strangest is the anglerfish. There are lots of different species of anglerfish, and all of them look like something out of a horror movie. Female anglerfish have enormous mouths studded with teeth and a glowing lure that sticks out of the top of their heads. The female anglerfish stays perfectly still in the water, waving its lure back and forth. The glowing lure flickers on and off so it looks a bit like a firefly, and attracts other fish right to the anglerfish's mouth.

Male anglerfish are even stranger than the females. Males are much smaller, completely black, and shaped like a finger. As they grow, the male's digestive system shuts down. By the time the male anglerfish is old enough to reproduce, he has to find a female in order to survive, or he'll die of starvation. When he finds a female, the male angler uses his tiny, hook-like teeth to bite a hole in her skin. Then his saliva eats away both the female's skin and the skin of the male's mouth so that they fuse together. For the rest of their lives both fish are attached together, and the male survives by being fed through the female. Sometimes up to six males will attach themselves to a single female anglerfish.

FASCINATING FACT

Creatures live in every part of the ocean, even the deepest trenches. The deepest place a fish has ever been found was in the Puerto Rico Trench, which is 27,460 feet deep (8,372 meters). Even in the deepest part of the ocean, scientists find life: in 2005, scientists discovered a type of plankton living in the Challenger Deep off the island of Guam.

Sharks are also quite curious. A raft is an interesting new thing to check out in their territory. Usually after they've checked out the raft and discovered it's much larger than they are, they will leave it alone. Many survivors have found that large sharks simply liked to hang out under and around their raft, just like the other fish, and after awhile, they didn't even pay attention to them.

There are a few types of sharks that are known to be aggressive and have a reputation for attacking humans. Most people probably won't run into these sharks, but if you do, beware!

Shortfin mako: This is the fastest shark—it can swim up to 20 miles an hour! A favorite of sport fishermen because the sharks fight so hard when hooked, it is known for attacking boats. Wouldn't you, if you were being reeled in?

White-tipped shark: This shark is famous for attacking and eating shipwrecked sailors during World War II. It is unpredictable and fearless. White-tipped sharks usually stay in deep waters.

Tiger shark: Famous for eating anything, tiger sharks have been known to eat license plates, lumps of coal, cans of paint—even a drum set. They have jaws with super-elastic muscles so they can open their mouths and swallow big things.

Bull shark: This shark is unusual because it can live in both salt and fresh water.

Great white shark: This shark has a terrible reputation, mostly based on the movie *Jaws*. The great white shark is responsible for most attacks on humans. Scientists think that the great white doesn't attack people on purpose. The shark is just curious and bites people to see if they might make a good meal, but one bite usually tells the shark that humans are too bony.

The problem for us is that one bite from a great white is more than enough to do a lot of damage—a great white can take in 20 to 30 pounds (9–13 kilograms) in a single bite.

THE SIMPLEST BUT DEADLIEST OCEAN CREATURE

There are creatures that are more dangerous than sharks but that you may never even see until it's too late: jellyfish. There are more than 2,000 different species of jellyfish, or jellies, as they are sometimes called, in oceans from the tropics to the poles. Jellies range in size from the tiny (less than an inch or 1 centimeter long) to the enormous (more than 200 feet, or 61 meters). Jellies are one of the simplest animals in the sea. They have no brains, hearts, lungs, eyes, or ears. They don't even have any bones! Jellyfish are basically floating eating machines. They have a stomach and small intestine, a mouth, and an anus. They also have thousands of stinging cells that are attached to tentacles that hang down from their bodies. Jellies catch their prey by bumping into it. The collision sets off an explosion of stinging cells. If what the jellyfish touches is small enough, the stinging cells will kill it and the jelly will have a meal.

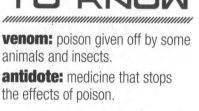

Most jellies aren't harmful to humans, even if they pack a painful sting. In fact, of the 2,000 jelly species in the world's oceans, only 70 kinds are dangerous to people. But those that are dangerous can be deadly. The most dangerous jelly of all is also the smallest: the Irukandji jelly, found in the tropical waters off northern Australia. The Irukandji is considered one of the deadliest creatures on Earth, mostly because its **venom** is incredibly powerful and has no **antidote**. One sting from an Irukandji can kill an adult human.

The scariest part about the Irukandji is that it is only about the size of a thumbnail and is completely transparent. The Irukandji is shaped like a little box and has a single, long tentacle hanging from each of its four corners. Several people die each year from Irukandji stings. Scientists think global warming will increase the range of Irukandji jellies throughout the tropical waters of the world.

WORDS TO KNOW

venom: poison given off by some animals and insects.
antidote: medicine that stops the effects of poison.

THE FUTURE OF THE OCEANS: MAKING CENSUS OF THE SEA

Our oceans are so big and still such a mystery that no one really knows how many species of plants and animals live there. So in 2000, scientists from 53 countries around the world began a giant project to find and name every single plant and animal in the world's oceans. Called the Census of Marine Life (www.coml.org), its goal is to spend 10 years counting as many different species as possible. Different teams from around the world have different areas to cover, ranging from deep-sea ridges to coral reefs.

Over the years that scientists have been working together on the **census**, many of their questions have changed. They want to do more than just count the number of species of animals and plants in an area. Scientists also want to know why those kinds of species are there at all, how they behave, and how the different species interact with each other.

Scientists have not only discovered some incredible new species of sea creatures—including sponges that eat meat—but have also learned things about sea creature behavior that they never knew before. By the time the survey is completed in 2010, scientists hope to have a better understanding not only of how many different kinds of animals and plants live in the ocean, but how all of these creatures will respond to changes in our climate. Some amazing highlights of the most recent survey report, finished in 2006 and published in 2007, are:

The oldest: In the Coral Sea, part of the southwestern Pacific Ocean, shrimp thought to have been extinct for more than 50 million years are alive and well, living deep underwater.

The most: Researchers using sonar off the New Jersey coast found a school of eight million herring. It covered an area the size of Manhattan!

WORDS TO KNOW

census: a gathering of data.

The newest: During three cruises off Antarctica, researchers trawling the bottom of the Southern Ocean discovered more new species in their trawl nets than species they already knew about!

The hottest: Scientists measuring temperatures near the thermal vents under the Atlantic Ocean near the equator found shrimp living near a vent that had a temperature of 765 degrees Fahrenheit (407 degrees Celsius). That's hot enough to melt lead.

The strangest: Near Easter Island (in the South Pacific), researchers discovered a crab completely covered in what looks like fur living in heat vents. They named the crab *Kiwa hirsuta*. *Kiwa* is the Polynesian goddess of shellfish. *Hirsuta* means "hairy."

Kiwa hirsuta

The Amazing, Ancient Coelacanth

The Indian Ocean is home to an incredible creature, the coelacanth, a fish that was thought to be extinct for 65 million years! In 1938, a local fisherman in southern Africa caught a strange-looking fish in his nets off the Comoros Islands and showed it to a local museum curator who liked looking at unusual fish. She realized that this fish was unlike any modern fish she'd ever seen, so she drew a picture of it and sent the picture to a famous **ichthyologist**. That scientist confirmed that the fish in the drawing was a prehistoric fish that had swum in the oceans during the age of the dinosaurs. The discovery made news all over the world—but the people of the Comoros Islands didn't know what the big fuss was all about. They caught coelacanths regularly. In fact, the fish were so common that people used their rough skin for sandpaper!

Coelacanth

WORDS TO KNOW

ichthyologist: a scientist who studies fish.

CHAPTER 3

The Ocean Food Web

All life in the ocean is linked together by food—all creatures eat, and some creatures get eaten. You probably already know that food chains are the links between food and the creatures that eat the food. Almost all food chains begin with plants. Small creatures eat the plants, and those creatures are eaten by slightly larger creatures. Then those creatures are eaten by larger creatures, and so on. Humans are at the top of the world's food chains.

Because the ocean is so huge and home to so many different kinds of living creatures, it doesn't have a single food chain. Instead, the ocean has many, many different food chains that are all connected to each other. Scientists call these interconnected food chains the ocean food web.

All ocean food chains start with the tiny, one-celled marine plants called phytoplankton. Phytoplankton float on or near the surface of the sunny, top layer of the ocean and use the sun's energy for photosynthesis. You probably remember that photosynthesis is the process that all green plants use to turn carbon dioxide and water into food.

Those phytoplankton are the first link in the food chain. They are eaten by tiny ocean animals called **zooplankton** (*zoo* means "animal" in Greek). Most zooplankton don't really swim; instead, they float in the top layer of the water and move with the currents. There are lots of different kinds of zooplankton, and they range in size from microscopic, single-celled creatures to small jellyfish. The tiniest zooplankton get eaten by slightly larger animals, which get eaten by even larger ones. The largest zooplankton, such as jellyfish, get eaten by lots of different kinds of small fish and other sea creatures, which then, in turn, are another ocean creature's meal.

WORDS TO KNOW

zooplankton: tiny ocean animals, like some jellyfish.
apex: the top point.

At the top of the ocean's food chains are **apex** predators: creatures with few or no natural enemies that prey on them. These include the largest game fish, such as billfish, swordfish, and tuna, as well as sharks, giant squid, and whales.

Some ocean food chains are very short and others are more complicated. One of the largest fish in the ocean, the basking shark, eats only the smallest creatures: zooplankton. The basking shark will swim through a cloud of zooplankton, open its enormous mouth, and suck in hundreds of thousands of zooplankton as it filters water through its gills.

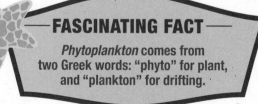

FASCINATING FACT

Phytoplankton comes from two Greek words: "phyto" for plant, and "plankton" for drifting.

Other food chains are much longer. A killer whale, for example, is at the top of a food chain that starts with plankton. Zooplankton such as krill eat the plankton. Small sea creatures such as herring or squid eat the krill. Larger fish such as tuna or snappers eat the smaller fish. Perhaps a seal or shark will eat those larger fish, and finally the killer whale eats the largest of these.

The reason scientists consider the ocean food system a web rather than a chain is that many different kinds of ocean creatures eat the same kinds of ocean food, and many of the same kinds of creatures eat each other, as well. A squid, for example, might eat many different types of fish, but it also will eat smaller squid.

FASCINATING FACT

There are lots of different sizes of zooplankton, ranging from the microscopic (called picoplankton) to those that are up to 8 inches (20 centimeters) long (called megaplankton). But zooplankton are divided into two different groups. One group will eventually grow and change into worms, shrimps, mollusks, crabs, coral, and fishes. The other kind of zooplankton doesn't change into any other creatures. They remain zooplankton their entire lives.

GLOBAL WARMING AFFECTS THE START OF THE OCEAN FOOD WEB

When the climate gets warmer, it affects the ocean's food web in more ways than you might think. Warmer temperatures are causing two major problems for the tiniest and most important links in the ocean food web. Scientists have discovered that when the ocean temperatures get too high, phytoplankton bloom less—as much as 30 percent less—than when the temperatures are cooler.

If the ocean temperatures continue to rise, scientists worry that the amount of phytoplankton in the world's oceans will decrease to dangerous lows. Another problem with warming temperatures

WORDS TO KNOW

Sahara Desert: the largest desert in the world, located in northern Africa.

is that it causes zooplankton to begin hatching before the phytoplankton are blooming. That means trouble for the food chain, too, because the zooplankton eat the phytoplankton. If their food source isn't available, the zooplankton could die off. That would affect all the other links in the food web.

— FASCINATING FACT —

A basking shark can filter more than 330,000 gallons (1.5 million liters) of water an hour while it is feeding.

DIFFERENT OCEAN ECOSYSTEMS

Did you know that some parts of the ocean have more life than others? Just as there are deserts with very little wildlife and tropical rainforests full of life on land, the ocean has areas that are rich in all kinds of sea life as well as areas that are almost like watery deserts. Currents, wind, saltiness, and sunlight all affect the amount of life in different parts of the ocean.

The Sahara Desert Fertilizes Plankton!

Scientists have recently discovered that giant dust storms that blow off the **Sahara Desert** in Africa are helping to create huge blooms of ocean plankton in the eastern Atlantic. The Saharan dust has lots of nitrogen, iron, and phosphorus in it, which acts like fertilizer for the plankton, making them grow and reproduce like crazy. Scientists are studying the ocean where the dust lands to see what effects it has on the food chain where the plankton blooms grow. About 500 million tons of dust gets blown off the Sahara and over the oceans each year, adding nutrients and even metals that are common on land but scarce in the water.

Areas rich in wildlife and areas almost empty of sea creatures can be relatively close to each other. Maralyn and Maurice Bailey discovered this when they were shipwrecked. The Baileys were sailing for the Galapagos Islands in the Pacific Ocean when a sperm whale smashed a huge hole in their sailboat. The boat sank in less than an hour, and Maralyn and Maurice had to scramble on board a 5-foot open rubber raft with only four containers of water and a small bag of food. They figured they could last for up to 20 days with their stored food if they collected rainwater, and they felt confident that they'd be rescued by then. But they weren't.

Maralyn and Maurice drifted in the open ocean for 117 days—that's almost four months! They traveled more than 1,500 miles (2,414 kilometers) before they were rescued by a Korean fishing boat. They survived because their boat sank in a part of the Pacific Ocean called the tropical convergence. In the tropical convergence a cold deepwater current comes up and mixes with the surface layer of the warm tropical ocean. The combination of the warm and cold water creates a place where there is lots and lots of sea life and regular rainfall. The Baileys were able to catch and eat all sorts of fish, turtles, and even seabirds, and they collected rainwater pretty regularly. While they lost 40 pounds (18 kilograms) each and were covered in sunburn and saltwater sores, they were in surprisingly good health when they were rescued. If they had been shipwrecked only a few hundred miles south (just one or two sailing days away), they would have been stuck in the middle of the tropical ocean, where the warm waters don't support as much sea life.

—FASCINATING FACT—
The name *copepod* comes from the Greek words for "oar" and "foot," so *copepod* means "oar-footed."

The Incredible Copepod

You might not believe it, but one of the most important creatures in the ocean is also the tiniest. Copepods are tiny creatures that live in both fresh and salt water and usually aren't more than about 1 millimeter long—although some can grow as long as 8 inches (20 centimeters)! Copepods are crustaceans, which means they have a shell, two antenna, and a segmented body. They are sometimes called the insects of the sea because there are more than 10,000 different species, and they are by far the biggest source of **protein** in the world's oceans. Copepods stay the same all their lives—they can get big, but they won't change into any other creature. Some copepods are parasites, which means they survive by feeding off a host without helping the host in any way. Almost all fish found in temperate and polar waters eat copepods at some point in their life cycle, and copepods also help feed fish and other creatures that live in the deep ocean waters. When copepods die, their hard shells (called exoskeletons) drift down to deep waters, where bottom dwellers like sea stars, urchins, sea cucumbers, and other creatures eat them.

Tropical Oceans: Many Kinds, Small Numbers

You might think that the warm, tropical oceans where the water temperatures are over 69 degrees Fahrenheit (20 degrees Celsius) all the time would be full of sea life. And you'd be right—sort of. Tropical oceans do have lots of different kinds of sea creatures, but not very many of each kind.

In the open tropical ocean there aren't many fish or sea creatures because there isn't much plankton. Low levels of plankton mean the warm water doesn't have many nutrients and can only support a small number of each kind of fish. Large fish tend to just pass through tropical waters on their way to better feeding grounds. Most of the life in tropical waters centers around coral reefs.

Coral reefs are organized ecosystems where competition for food is fierce. Each kind of fish or plant that lives on a coral reef has a specific food it eats, and a job it does to help another species survive and thrive.

WORDS TO KNOW

protein: a compound found in many foods such as meat and eggs that we and other animals need to survive.

For example, you'll find cleaning stations on coral reefs. These are places where tiny fish called wrasses pick off parasites, food scraps, and dead scales from larger fish, including sharks and moray eels. These little fish will even go in and out of large fish's mouths to clean them. Normally the larger fish would eat the smaller ones, but at the cleaning stations the small fish know they are safe. The wrasses get almost all of their food from cleaning larger fish, and the larger fish stay healthy because parasites, dead scales, and other stuff gets cleaned away.

WORDS TO KNOW

Endangered Species Act: an act passed by Congress designed to protect plants and animals from extinction.

The Green Sea Turtle

The green sea turtle is the largest hard-shelled turtle in the ocean. It can grow to be 3 feet (almost a meter) long and weigh between 300 and 350 pounds (136 to 159 kilograms). Green sea turtles nest on tropical and subtropical beaches all over the world. They are the only sea turtles that are vegetarians as adults. When they reach adulthood, they move from the open ocean close to shore and live on algae and sea grass. Green turtles have been eaten by native peoples for centuries, and were also regularly caught by sailing ships and whaling boats for food. Sailors would keep the turtles alive on the decks of their ships for months, saving them to eat when their other food ran out. So many turtles were hunted for food, in fact, that they were one of the first animals protected under the **Endangered Species Act** in 1973, but they are still hunted today.

Temperate Oceans: Populations Depend on the Seasons

Temperate oceans are areas that have water temperatures between 40 and 67 degrees Fahrenheit (5–18 degrees Celsius). That's a big temperature difference, and it's caused by the changing seasons and variations in the amount of sunlight. Temperate oceans can get as little as four hours of sunlight per day in the winter. Little sunlight means less plant life. When the plankton are gone, many fish migrate to other areas of the ocean, following the sun to find food. In the summer, though, the temperate oceans can get as many as 20 hours of sunlight. Nutrients washed into the oceans by rivers combined with all that summer sunlight makes the plankton bloom like crazy. When plankton bloom, lots of animals on the food chain follow, and the waters are chock-full of fish and other sea creatures.

Cold Oceans: Lots of the Same Kinds of Creatures

Cold-water oceans, with water temperatures of up to 40–50 degrees Fahrenheit (5–10 degrees Celsius), are kind of the opposite of tropical oceans. They have lots of sea life, but large numbers of only a few different kinds. In some places, the sea creatures exist nowhere else on Earth. In the coldest ocean waters of Antarctica, plants and animals have adapted to life where it is cold all the time. Some Arctic and Antarctic animals, such as whales and sea-birds, migrate to warmer places during the coldest parts of the year, but other sea creatures, such as sea stars, crabs, and polar seals, live in the polar water year-round.

FINDING FOOD IN THE OCEAN

Sea creatures spend all of their time searching for food, or trying to avoid being food for something else. But imagine you are suddenly shipwrecked in the open ocean and you need to find food? You will have to spend all of your time searching for it, too. And your success will depend a lot on where in the world's oceans you are. You already know about the ocean's food webs, and which kinds of ocean creatures are more likely to be in warm, tropical waters than in temperate or cold waters. So how will you catch enough food to eat?

Narwhals

Narwhals, relatives of bottlenose dolphins and orcas, are known as the unicorns of the sea—and with good reason. Male narwhals grow a spiraling tusk that can be as long as 8.75 feet (2.5 meters) ! The tusk is really one of the narwhal's two teeth and grows right through its upper lip. Scientists aren't really sure why narwhals grow such a long tusk, but they think it has to do with attracting mates. Years ago, scientists thought narwhals used their tusks to spear fish, but it turns out that's not true. Female narwhals sometimes grow short tusks, but never as long as males. Narwhals live only in the coldest waters of the Arctic. Like their dolphin cousins, narwhals usually hunt their prey of small fish, shrimp, and other sea animals in packs of 15 to 20, but there have been reports of hundreds—and even thousands—of narwhals swimming together in the ocean.

TRY THIS: ESTIMATE HOW MANY CALORIES A DAY YOU EAT

Try to track the number of calories you eat for one regular day. For one day, write down everything you eat, and about how much of it you eat. You can find how many calories are in the average serving of most foods by looking on the package. For example, if you eat a bowl of cereal with milk, the nutrition information on the side of the box will tell you how many calories you've just eaten. Compare the number of calories you eat with the number of calories your body needs based on the *Try This* on page 40.

Dead Zones

There are parts of the ocean where there is no life at all. These dead zones are caused by something called *anoxia*, which means "no oxygen." When the phytoplankton that bloom on the surface of the ocean sink to the bottom, they are eaten by bacteria. It seems like this would be a good thing. But the problem is that the bacteria use oxygen and make carbon dioxide in the process. If the bacteria take so much oxygen from the water that nothing else can live—the oxygen in the water disappears. These dead zones are growing in different areas of the ocean, especially in places where big rivers flow into the oceans. These are places where plankton is abundant. Scientists think fertilizer from farms gets into the rivers and then flows into the ocean. Fertilizer has nutrients that make plants grow faster, but phytoplankton grow faster, too, when fertilized.

—FASCINATING FACT—
The Gulf of Mexico dead zone, where the Mississippi River flows into the ocean, is one of the largest dead zones in the world.

try this: HOW Many Calories DO YOU NeeD a Day?

If you're lost at sea, you're obviously not worrying about how many calories a day you're eating—unless you're not getting enough. But in everyday life it can be easy to eat more calories than your body needs to stay healthy. Here's an easy way to figure out about how many calories you should eat a day to maintain a healthy body weight. If you are very active (play a lot outside, do sports, or exercise every day), multiply your body weight by 20. That will give you a rough estimate of the number of calories you should eat. If you are moderately active (play outside every day, but do sports or exercise only a couple of days a week), multiply your body weight by 17. If you are sedentary, which means you really don't exercise or play outside very much, multiply your body weight by 14. This will give you the number of calories you should be eating.

HOW TO FISH

Depending on where you are in the world, you will be able to find different types of food. In spring in the temperate or cold-water oceans, for example, you will likely be able to find clouds of plankton. They float on the surface, often in sort of jelly-like blobs, and you can often scoop them up and strain them through your clothes. They may not taste like much, but they will help give you some much-needed nutrition, including vitamins. In temperate oceans, you are more likely to find fish and turtles, and in some places, you can collect seaweed.

In some parts of the ocean, you could have trouble finding much food at all because of the combination of currents, saltiness of the water, and temperature. If you're in a tropical ocean, for example, you may have a hard time finding food in deep water, since most fish use tropical oceans as highways to other places. No matter where you are, though, your best sources of food will be fish, and your best method for catching them will be fishing.

You can fish in many different ways, depending on what supplies you have on hand. You can catch fish on a line, scoop them in a net, spear them, or gaff them with a hook. Which method works for you will depend on what supplies you have and how strong you are.

Line Fishing

If you want to catch fish on a line, you'll need a hook, bait, and some kind of line—it can be anything from a proper fishing line to a sail sheet to strips of

cloth from your clothes or even your shoelaces. You can make hooks from whatever sharp piece of metal you have. If you have a safety pin, that will work. If you have a knife blade, or even a small piece of metal, you can bend it and tie it onto your line and be good to go. Bait can be any food you might have that will stay on the hook under water. Keep in mind that most fish will only eat other fish or meat. If you don't have any food for bait, you can attach small pieces of metal to your line that might attract fish—buttons, belt buckles, or even the metal eyes from shoes can all work.

It's easy to make a fishing line. You simply wrap the line several times around your hook, tie a strong knot, and throw the line over the side. You'll have the best luck trying to snag a small fish that you can then cut up for bait.

The most important thing to remember about creating a fishing line is that you should never wrap the line around your hands. It sounds pretty dumb, but there are several reasons for this. When seawater evaporates,

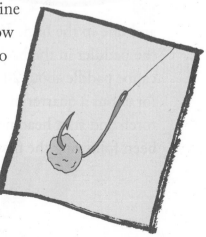

Spear Fishing

To spear a fish, remember that when light passes through water, it bends. That's because water is a different density than air. That means that when you look at a fish from above the surface of the water, the fish isn't really where you see it. It is almost always slightly lower in the water than where it seems. Even if you are looking straight down at the fish you are trying to spear, it will look bigger and closer to the surface than it actually is. If you are looking at the fish from an angle, such as behind or in front, aim your spear behind and below where you think the fish is swimming. Spearing fish takes practice and can be really challenging, especially if you're trying to balance over the side of a raft and hold onto the line at the same time. If you can get the hang of estimating the difference between where the fish looks like it is swimming and where it actually is, it's much easier.

— FASCINATING FACT —

Tahitian fishermen use a special kind of boat called a *poti marara* that has a steering stick in the front. The captain can steer the boat with one hand and spear fish alongside the boat with the other.

TRY THIS: MAKE A FISHING SPEAR

Making a double-pronged spear is actually pretty easy. Find a long, straight sapling. Split one end of the sapling about 6 inches (15 centimeters) down the middle. Then push a small wood chip into the split to spread apart the two halves of the sapling. Sharpen those two ends into points. If you are practicing in deep water, tie a line around the top of the spear so you can retrieve it after you've thrown it.

FISH TO AVOID

While you may be so hungry that you don't particularly care what kind of fish you eat, you should know that some fish can make you sick—and some can even kill you. Most fish that you find in the open ocean are fine to eat, but if you are in shallow water near coral reefs, be careful. Some algae that grow on coral reefs are poisonous to humans. Fish eat the toxic algae, and the toxins stay in their flesh. The more algae the fish eat, the more toxic they become. Some fish that can live in the open ocean, such as barracuda, are not safe to eat if caught near a reef. In general, the most poisonous kinds of fish usually have rounded bodies with shell-like skins covered in spines. They also usually have small, parrot-like mouths. Porcupine fish, trigger fish, and puffer fish are definitely fish to avoid.

Puffer Fish—Dangerous Delicacy

Puffer fish, also known as blowfish, are small fish that live in the tropical Pacific that can inflate themselves when they feel threatened. Predators have a hard time swallowing a fish the shape and size of a mini beach ball. But the puffer fish's best protection is its poison. Puffer fish are very poisonous—in fact, there is enough poison in one puffer fish to kill 30 people, and there is no antidote. But this super-toxic fish is also a super-expensive and much-loved food in Asia. People in Japan pay big bucks to eat puffer fish sushi, which is called fugu. The fish is prepared only by special chefs who are trained and licensed by the government to be able to prepare fugu. The chefs have to take both a written test and eat the fugu they have prepared in order to get their license. Even so, more than 100 people die each year after eating the fish.

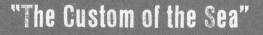

"The Custom of the Sea"

During the eighteenth and nineteenth centuries ships were the most common way of long-distance travel. Shipwrecks were much more common than they are today, and sailors who were shipwrecked often found themselves floating in small boats for weeks at a time with almost no supplies and with little hope of rescue. Sometimes the shipwrecked sailors would grow so desperate for food and water that they would eat the bodies of shipmates who died on board the life rafts.

When that food source was gone, sailors would resort to another terrible way to survive that became known as "the custom of the sea." Survivors would draw lots to see who would be sacrificed so the other survivors could eat their flesh and drink their blood and stay alive for a bit longer. Cannibalism at sea was actually fairly common for centuries, and many stories, songs, and jokes of the time mention it.

In fact, sometimes sailors who had eaten human flesh for survival were paid to come on stage as part of traveling freak shows. One of the most famous stories of "the custom of the sea" happened in 1820, when the whaling ship *Essex* was attacked by a giant sperm whale in the Pacific Ocean. In only 15 minutes, the ship sank and her crew was left adrift in three small whaling boats with no supplies. They drifted for more than three months, and resorted to "the custom of the sea," killing the cabin boy for food and eatng other crew members when they died.

When the survivors of the *Essex* finally made it to shore and told their story, it became famous. In fact, a young whaler and writer named Herman Melville who had heard the story wrote a book about it. Its name? *Moby Dick*.

CHAPTER 4

Seafaring and Ocean Exploration

Oceans are our planet's largest **habitat**—but they are also the least explored. Even though more than 70 percent of our planet is under water, less than 5 percent of the ocean habitat has ever been seen by humans.

People have been sailing on the world's oceans for thousands of years. More than 5,000 years ago the ancient Egyptians kept records of their sea voyages. Other ocean-going civilizations included the Greeks, Phoenicians, and Romans. The **Phoenicians** traveled all the way from the Mediterranean to the Atlantic Ocean to trade with countries in western Africa as early as 1250 BCE. That's more than 3,000 years ago!

47

But the most amazing ocean travelers were the ancient Polynesians. They traveled all over the Pacific Ocean as early as 1500 BCE, settling islands up to 4,000 miles (6,437 kilometers) from where they started. The Polynesians sailed in huge wooden canoes, guided only by the stars, and brought rocks with them to make tools once they arrived at their new destination. They passed their knowledge of the wind, stars, and ocean from generation to generation, until about 550 years ago. Then it seems that their explorations stopped. Scientists don't know why.

European and Asian explorers traveled the world's oceans over the next 400 years, learning new trade routes and exploring other continents for land and wealth. Today, all of the world's oceans have been explored—at least on the surface. Exploration below the waves is an entirely different story.

WORDS TO KNOW

habitat: the environment or place where an organism or group of organisms lives.

Phoenicians: a civilization located on the shores of North Africa and the eastern Mediterranean Sea around the year 1000 BCE.

nautical mile: a measurement of distance used on the ocean (6,082 feet or 1,853 meters) that is longer than a regular land mile.

THE MYSTERIOUS DEEP OCEAN

Why do we know so little about the ocean floor? For thousands of years, people sailed on the oceans but didn't know exactly where they were at any given time. Early sailors navigated only by the stars. They could get where they were going, but couldn't pinpoint exactly where they were on the ocean. If you don't know where you are on top of the water, you can't know where you are underneath, either. And most people in the world believed that the oceans were too cold, too deep, and way too dark for anything to live more than a few hundred feet beneath the surface. They viewed the deep water of the oceans as black and empty.

Another major problem with exploring under the ocean's surface is that most humans can only stay underwater without breathing for about 3 minutes. So for centuries the only view people had of the world under the ocean's surface was of the fish and sea creatures that fishermen pulled up with their nets. The deep sea was a world that remained a complete mystery.

FASCINATING FACT

We have only explored about 10 percent of the deep ocean floor and have 1,860,000 square miles (300 million square kilometers) left to investigate.

THE FIRST UNDERSEA EXPLORERS

People have been experimenting with ways to breathe underwater for thousands of years. Aristotle, a famous Greek scientist, described how divers could turn over a container that was filled with air, stick their heads in, and breathe underwater. Over the centuries, many other scientists, including Leonardo da Vinci, tried different versions of this idea. In the early 1700s, an English scientist named Sir Edmond Halley (the guy who discovered the famous comet) built a diving bell that allowed divers to walk along the bottom of a shallow seabed while breathing air from a huge wooden container. The divers put a glass bell over their heads that was attached to a hose that led to the container. The container trapped air from the surface and allowed it to be pushed through the hose to the jar. Halley wasn't the first person to design diving equipment, but his diving bell made it possible for people to actually spend long periods of time underwater.

THE CHALLENGER EXPEDITION

By the mid 1800s, the world had changed enormously. It was a time of many new ideas and great exploration, and scientists began to think about exploring the world underneath the waves. In 1872, a British ship called the HMS *Challenger* set out on a mission around the world. The goal of the *Challenger* expedition was to learn about the ocean. The ship traveled 68,890 **nautical miles** over two years, measuring the depths of the oceans, collecting specimens of sea life, learning about ocean chemistry, and recording

water temperatures. They collected so much data that it took scientists more than 20 years to analyze it.

The *Challenger* expedition made people realize that perhaps the ocean wasn't just a giant, empty fishbowl. Instead, the discoveries made aboard the *Challenger* excited scientists, because they revealed that under all that water was a completely different world. The researchers discovered that underneath the waves there were huge mountain ranges, giant flat plains, ridges, and canyons. And when the *Challenger* crew brought up the nets that had been dragged along the seafloor, it pulled up creatures that lived in water that was previously thought to be far too deep to ever support life. The results of the *Challenger* expedition were the beginnings of the science of oceanography.

— FASCINATING FACT —

It wasn't until the mid 1700s that ships used **chronometers** (an accurate ship's clock) to help them pinpoint where they were on the globe using latitude and **longitude**.

TRY THIS: MAKE AN EASY DIVING BELL

The next time you're at the pool and have an adult around, you can see how a diving bell works. Take a bucket and tip it upside down quickly so that the mouth of the bucket is underwater but the rest of it is above water. Hold your breath and go underwater, surfacing with your head inside the bucket. You'll be able to breathe because the bucket has trapped air in it. Make sure you try this only when an adult is with you!

THE CHALLENGE OF DEEP WATER

The *Challenger* expedition opened a whole new world to science. One of the missions the *Challenger* faced was to make an accurate map of the seafloor. The *Challenger* took thousands of **soundings** of the seafloor, and made a map based on the measurements, but no one was sure what the seafloor—or the ocean waters more than a hundred feet deep—actually looked like, because no human could possibly dive that deep.

FASCINATING FACT

When the *Challenger* crew set out to make a map of the bottom of the Atlantic Ocean, they thought they might find Atlantis, a famous lost city.

Scientists spent years trying to create a special vehicle so people could explore the deep ocean. Those special vehicles came into being in the 1930s, with the invention of the bathysphere. It was a cast-iron, bubble-shaped diving bell, invented by a man named Otis Barton, that carried two men down to 3,000 feet (914 meters)—the deepest any human had ever been in the ocean. Over the next 40 years, other deep-sea vehicles followed the first bathysphere. Humans eventually dived down to 33,800 feet (11,000 meters), the bottom of the Mariana Trench, in a deep-sea vehicle called the *Trieste* in 1960. But as deep as this dive was, it still was only to one spot in the huge ocean.

WORDS TO KNOW

chronometer: an accurate clock used in navigation.

longitude: imaginary lines running through the north and south poles that indicate where you are on the globe.

sounding: measuring the depth of water.

As computer technology advanced, scientists were able to make underwater vehicles that they could steer by remote control. They call these ROVs, for "remotely operated vehicles." Scientists attach video cameras to the vehicles so they can see everything at the sea floor, just as if they are riding in them. These underwater vehicles can go all sorts of places that humans couldn't. ROVs are the new way that oceanographers explore the deep seas, and they have helped make some of the most amazing underwater discoveries of all time.

Bathysphere

Self-Contained Underwater Breathing Apparatus (SCUBA)

In 1945, oceanographers Jacques Cousteau and Emile Gagnan came up with an invention that would change underwater exploration forever. They called it a Self-Contained Underwater Breathing Apparatus, but we know it as the scuba tank. Scuba tanks attach to the back of a vest that divers put on like a coat. The scuba tank is filled with an air mixture that is held under pressure. The tank connects to a hose that is attached to a mouthpiece. When the diver breathes in through the mouthpiece, air is pulled from the tank. When the diver breathes out, the mouthpiece releases carbon dioxide back into the water. With a scuba tank, divers can swim freely wherever they want. The only constraints divers have with scuba tanks is the amount of time they can spend underwater and the depth they can safely dive to without other special equipment.

TRY THIS: MAKE YOUR OWN SOUNDING DEVICE

A sounding is a measurement of how deep water is. Early sailors would take soundings with a weight attached to a rope. They'd lower the weight over the side of a ship, letting out rope until the weight hit the bottom. Then they'd mark the spot on the rope at the water level, and after the weight was pulled to the surface, they'd measure the amount of rope from the mark to the weight. Today, sonar and other computer-aided technologies help make measuring the depth of deep water much simpler. If you have a community pool, try seeing how accurate your sounding methods are. Take a rope or some kind of line and tie a weight to the bottom. Toss the line into the water and let out rope until the weight hits bottom. Mark the rope at the surface of the water, and then pull it up. Measure the amount of rope from the weight to the mark. Does it match up with the depth marker on the side of the pool?

HUMANS JUST CAN'T STAND THE PRESSURE

Humans are built for land, not water. Air is a lot lighter than water—almost 1,000 times lighter, in fact. A liter of air weighs about 0.04 ounces (1.2 grams). One liter of water weighs about 2.2 pounds (1,000 grams). When we are standing on land, we don't even feel the pressure of the air around us. But when we go into water, that changes. When you go underwater, you have the weight of water pushing down on you from all sides. The deeper you go, the more weight pushes on you. You've probably felt this when you try to dive to the bottom of the deep end of a pool. The pressure you feel is **hydrostatic pressure**—it's the weight of all that water pushing on you from all sides.

Every time you go 33 feet (10 meters) deeper, the pressure pushing on you increases by one atmosphere. An atmosphere is the normal air pressure around you on land. At 33 feet (10 meters) underwater the pressure on your body is twice as much as it is on land. That isn't too bad. But at 66 feet (20 meters), it's three times as much pressure as on land. And as you go deeper, the pressure on your body increases more and more, and it gets harder for your organs to work properly. The pressure squishes your lungs, heart, and other organs so they have to work extra hard to move the oxygen through your blood.

Humans can't dive deeper than about 400 feet (120 meters) without a special suit, because our lungs just can't move air properly at that depth. And even with special suits, humans can't dive below about 2,000 feet (600 meters) unless they are inside a special vehicle. Otherwise you'd be squished as flat as a pancake.

WORDS TO KNOW

hydrostatic pressure: the measure of the pressure at a given depth underwater.

CHAPTER 5

Ocean Navigators

For thousands of years, people have used the day and night sky to navigate the oceans. If they wanted to find east, ancient sailors would watch where the sun rose. If they wanted to find west, they'd watch where the sun set. This simple method of navigation might not have given early sailors an exact east or west heading, because the sun only rises precisely in the east and sets precisely in the west in certain places at certain times of the year. But it gave them a general sense of direction and helped them stay on course. Once a sailor has figured out which directions are east and west, north and south can also be identified.

Sailors today still can use sky navigation to help them know where they are at sea. Think about what Dougal Robinson and his family did when their sailboat was crushed by a pod of whales near the Galapagos Islands and sank in less than a minute. The family crowded into a life raft with no instruments of any kind, and only enough food and water to last three days. But Dougal knew enough about the sun, stars, and ocean currents to try to steer for Costa Rica, which he estimated was probably about 50 days away. After 37 days at sea, the Robinsons were rescued by a Japanese fishing boat. But what was really amazing was that the Robinsons were only 290 miles (467 kilometers) from the exact location they had been steering toward! Dougal didn't have much control over how fast or far his raft floated on the water, but he knew he needed to keep heading east in order to make it to land. So the family always made sure their raft was heading in an easterly direction while they were at sea, and they traveled 1,000 miles (1,609 kilometers) across the Pacific Ocean, heading right for their intended landing point. Pretty impressive.

TRY THIS: MAKE A SIMPLE COMPASS

You'll need a cork, magnet, and sewing needle to make a simple and fairly accurate compass. Here's how: take the magnet (a bar magnet works best but a refrigerator magnet will also work) and rub it in one direction along the needle. Do this about 10 times. This will magnetize the needle a bit. Now take the piece of cork and push the needle through it so both ends of the needle are sticking out of the cork. Place the cork with the needle in it in a small saucer of water. The floating needle will point to magnetic north!

STARS AS COMPASS POINTS

The stars have been used by sailors for navigation for as long as there have been ships on the water. The true masters of using the stars were the Polynesians. The Polynesians memorized star patterns and used them as nighttime compasses, then passed down the information from generation to generation. The sailors would use between seven and twelve of the brightest and most distinct stars in the night sky as their compass. Here's how it worked: the navigator would steer the canoe toward the brightest star on the **horizon**. When that star set below the horizon or rose too high to be useful as a guide, he'd use the next one, and so on until the sun rose. Then he'd carefully note the position of the canoe compared to where the sun rose, and later, where the sun set. That way he'd always know exactly where his canoe was when night fell again.

If you are in the Northern Hemisphere, you can use one of the brightest stars in the sky as a compass, too. Polaris, also known as the North Star, will help you find north. Polaris is directly above the North Pole, and lines up with the earth's **axis**. It looks like the only star in the night sky of the Northern Hemisphere that doesn't move (of course none of the stars are moving—the earth is moving around its axis).

If you were standing on the North Pole, Polaris would be directly above you. If you watched the sky all night, all of the stars in the night sky would look as if they are moving around Polaris as the earth rotates.

WORDS TO KNOW

horizon: the point in the distance where the sky and the earth seem to meet.

axis: the center, around which something rotates.

constellation: a group of stars in the sky that resembles a certain shape, such as the Big Dipper.

Try This: Find Polaris

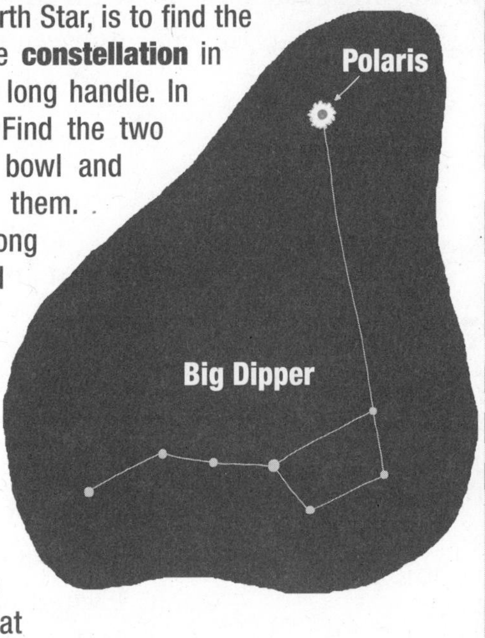

The easiest way to find Polaris, the North Star, is to find the Big Dipper first. The Big Dipper is the **constellation** in the sky that looks like a bowl with a long handle. In England it is known as the Plough. Find the two stars that make the outside of the bowl and draw an imaginary line between them. Extend that line about five times as long as the line between the two stars and you'll run right into Polaris.

You can find south if you are in the Southern Hemisphere by using the Southern Cross, or Crux, as your guide. This constellation is made up of five bright stars that form a cross that tilts to one side. The two stars that make up the cross's long arm are the pointer stars. To find south, look at the distance between the two pointer stars. Now add an imaginary line about five times as long as the line between the two pointer stars. Look straight down to the horizon from where that imaginary line ends. That is just about due south. It can be a little tricky at sea, where there are no landmarks to use as a guide, but by following the long arm of the Southern Cross down and then dropping an imaginary line to the horizon, you'll get a sense of where south is.

Polaris

Big Dipper

— FASCINATING FACT —

There is no single star called the South Star that can help you find south. That is because there is not a bright star lined up with the earth's axis in the south.

CURRENTS—OCEAN WATER ON THE MOVE

When you are on the ocean, you're on the move all the time. Ocean waters are always moving, pushed by the wind and pulled by gravity and the spinning of the earth. Huge amounts of water move in the same direction, at the same speed, all the time, like giant rivers flowing in different parts of the ocean. These are called currents, and they carry water all over the world.

Surface ocean currents are formed mostly by the sun and wind. The sun heats the surface of the earth, causing hot air to rise and colder air to rush in to take the hot air's place. The cold air moving over the top of the water causes friction between itself and the water. That friction is energy, and makes the water move.

Land masses also help shape ocean currents, because they affect the direction of the winds that move the water. Even the earth's rotation helps to direct ocean currents. Because the earth is always spinning, everything on it is spinning, too, including the water in the oceans and the winds that direct the water. This causes the ocean currents to move in giant circular patterns.

Each major ocean **basin** has currents that move in these circular patterns, which are called gyres. Gyres move in a clockwise direction in the Northern Hemisphere and counterclockwise in the Southern Hemisphere—except near the poles. Gyres tend to flow in the opposite direction near the poles.

Ocean currents can move at speeds of up to about 6 miles (10 kilometers) an hour. That may not seem fast, but remember that ocean currents never stop moving.

WORDS TO KNOW

basin: a natural depression in the surface of land or underwater.

nutrients: a source of nourishment for animals and plants, found in food.

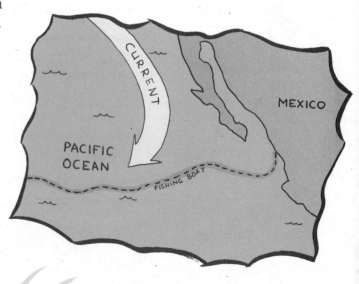

Over time, you could go a pretty long way without even realizing you're moving very much. That's what happened to three Mexican fishermen in 2006. They set out off the Pacific coast of Mexico for a short sharkfishing trip, but lost their engine soon after they had left port. They were pushed out to sea by high winds and caught by a current. It took nine months for them to be rescued, and when they were, the fishermen discovered that their boat had been swept 5,500 miles (8,851 kilometers) across the Pacific Ocean!

Surface currents are really important not only for sailors, who can use the currents to move across the oceans faster and more efficiently, but also to the world's climate and the ocean's health. Currents help spread energy and heat from the sun throughout the waters of the world. Surface currents move water from the tropics toward the poles, transferring heat to colder waters. Surface currents also help make room for cold-water upwelling. Warm water moves away from the surface by currents, allowing colder water from deeper in the ocean to come up. The colder water brings lots of **nutrients** with it. Those nutrients spark lots of plankton growth, which in turn helps feed ocean life.

The Trade Winds

Because the sun hits the earth's atmosphere most directly at the equator, the distance the sun's rays have to travel before they hit the surface of the earth is short. That means that lots of energy is transferred as heat. The air at the equator heats up really quickly, becomes less dense, and rises. Cooler air rushes in from other areas to fill the gap, creating wind. These winds around the equator are called the trade winds. They are very constant.

You might think it would make sense that the trade winds would blow south in the Northern Hemisphere, and north in the Southern Hemisphere, since cold air is rushing in to replace the hot air that rises. And they do. But the trade winds also blow from an easterly direction, too. Why? Because the earth is rotating all the time, and that means that every single thing on earth is moving with it.

Things in the Northern Hemisphere move to the right, while things in the Southern Hemisphere move to the left. Even the wind is affected by the rotation of the earth, which makes the trade winds blow slightly to the west, all the time. The trade winds are very constant. They are so constant, in fact, that for centuries sailors have used the trade winds as a reliable pathway across the oceans.

DEEP OCEAN CURRENTS

For centuries people thought that the only currents in the ocean were the ones on the surface. But scientists discovered that the deep ocean has currents, too—and those deep-ocean currents are incredibly important in maintaining the earth's climate.

Deep-ocean currents are formed by temperature differences and salt content. The denser and colder water is, the heavier it gets. So colder, denser water tends to sink. Water at the earth's poles has less salt and colder temperatures than water in other regions, so it sinks—sometimes all the way to the ocean floor. When that water sinks to the bottom, it travels from the polar regions along the bottom of the ocean back toward the equatorial regions, where it starts to get warmer. As it warms, it rises to replace water that is moving away at the surface.

You can think of the world's oceans as a giant bathtub: Picture two faucets—one near the North Pole, and one near the South Pole. The faucets are turned on all the time, filling the ocean with cold water from the bottom up. That's what is going on in the deep ocean, all the time. It is called **thermohaline** circulation, and it is really, really important to our planet's climate. Why?

Global Warming and Deep Ocean Currents

Some scientists worry that global warming could affect the Conveyor with drastic results. If ocean waters become less salty due to the melting of the polar ice caps, for example, they will be less dense. Less dense water has to be much cooler to sink. If the water can't sink, then the deep-water currents stop flowing. That means that the cold water circulation would stop. That would change the temperature of all the world's oceans—and our climate. Some scientists predict that if the Conveyor stopped, countries in northern Europe would grow much colder since the Atlantic Ocean would be most seriously affected.

Because it moves water to and from all different parts of the oceans, moving heat from warm places to cooler places, bringing oxygen from the surface to the depths, and constantly regulating the temperature of our planet. Scientists call all of these deep, connected currents the Conveyor, because together they move so much water around the world. It is a very slow process—the full cycle can take a thousand years to complete. Many scientists believe that it is vital to keeping our planet's climate stable.

WORDS TO KNOW

thermohaline: a type of current that moves vast amounts of water around the world.

global warming: an increase in the average temperature of the earth's atmosphere, causing climate change.

USING OCEAN CURRENTS TO KNOW WHERE YOU ARE

Most sailors today rely on GPS (global positioning systems) to navigate through the ocean's waters. They often don't know how to read the ocean itself for navigation clues. But the ocean's currents can tell you a lot about where you are and where you're going. You already know that ocean currents move all over the world, bringing warm water to colder regions, and cold water to warmer regions. But what you might not know is that you can often identify a surface current by the color of the water.

The color of the ocean tends to be greener when the water is colder. That's because colder water usually has more plankton in it. Why? Cold water usually has less salt content, so plankton can grow better. Plankton are green plants—more green plants mean more green water. Warmer water is usually blue because warmer ocean water generally has a higher salt content. The salt content is higher because warmer temperatures mean more water evaporation, taking away water but leaving salt behind. More salt means less plant growth. Less plant growth means bluer water.

So as a general rule, colder oceans are greener and tropical oceans are bluer. When cold currents come through warm, tropical water, or warm currents come through colder water, you can both see and feel the difference. The Gulf Stream, for example, is a fast, warm current that flows north from the straits of Mexico to the straits of Florida and northward up the eastern coast of the United States. It is very blue and has very little marine life in it. The Labrador Current is a very cold current that flows down from Greenland and the Canadian Arctic past the northeastern coast of North America.

This current is full of marine life and very green. When the Labrador Current and the Gulf Stream meet off the southern coast of North Carolina, the difference in color between the two currents is very clear. Even more extreme is the temperature difference: in places, the temperature of the water can drop or rise 30 degrees Fahrenheit (-1 degree Celsius) as you pass from one current to the other.

WORDS TO KNOW

Sargasso Sea: an area in the North Atlantic that is surrounded by currents but which has no currents of its own. It is full of seaweed and has very few living animals.

—FASCINATING FACT—
The **Sargasso Sea** in the tropical Atlantic Ocean is bluer and clearer than any other part of the ocean because it has so much salt and so little life in it.

Sometimes Green Water Means Land is Near

Not all green water is cold water. There are areas of green water in the tropical oceans too, usually near the mouths of large rivers. Dirt brought down from the river to its mouth fans out into the ocean, turning the water a muddy green. Some large rivers, such as the Amazon in South America, bring so much freshwater to the ocean that for miles out to sea the water is more fresh than salt. The freshwater makes plankton grow more in these places, turning the water green. So if you're in the tropics in deep water and the water is green, you may be closer to land than you think.

So if you were out at sea and noticed a major temperature difference in the water while the air temperature stayed the same, or you spotted a definite change in the color of the water, then you have probably come across a major current.

FINDING DIRECTION FROM WAVES AND SWELLS

No matter where you are in the world's oceans, there will be a predictable ocean swell underneath you. The movement of the waves tells you from what direction a constant, stable wind is coming. Swells are different from waves: they form as wind blows from one direction over long periods of time. Waves are created by surface winds, and can come from any direction for short periods of time. Even when the weather changes—if a storm comes, for example—and waves come from different directions, the swell will stay the same because it is formed by long-term wind patterns. That's why in stormy seas the waves seem to be coming from all different directions at the same time—because waves might be coming from a different direction than the swell. Swell patterns are a really good way to figure out what direction you're heading. Winds may change, but the direction of the swell won't.

Ocean Swells

Once you've figured out which direction the swell is heading, you can use it to stay on track no matter how the weather changes.

Even though waves aren't as predictable as ocean swells, they can also tell you a lot about what is going on around you. For example, they can help you find land that you can't see. If there is land with high ground near the shore and a wind is blowing off the land, the size of the waves will drop a lot, even if the wind is strong. So if you're on the water and notice that the wind is blowing steadily but the waves have become smaller, it's a pretty good indicator that land is in the direction the wind is coming from.

Ocean Navigators, Swells, and Waves

The Polynesians relied on swell patterns to navigate the Pacific Ocean. When bad weather made using the sky impossible for navigation, the Polynesians would use ocean swells as a compass instead. They would keep their canoes at an angle to the swells, knowing that the swells showed a particular direction. When their canoes made sudden changes in motion, like bumping against the swells rather than riding with them, the navigators knew that the canoe had changed course, and they would get it back on track. To avoid getting off course a lot, the navigator would attach a rope to the canoe to use as a path marker. If a sudden big wave pushed the canoe off course, the rope trailing behind would still be on the right course since it followed the swell. The men on the canoe could look at the position of the rope and reorient their canoes to the right direction.

The ancient Micronesians were so good at navigating by and understanding swell patterns that they made charts and maps of their local surface waters out of coconut palms and coconut fiber. The map makers would weave coconut ribs into the fiber to show the meeting points of dominant wave swells around the islands. They used small shells to show the network of islands the swells surrounded. Their charts were based on a time scale, not a distance scale—they measured distances in how many canoe days it would take to get from island to island, and they wove sticks into the charts to show the point at sea from which they could see the first palm tree on an island.

CHAPTER 6

Surviving Ocean Extremes

Think about how extreme an environment the ocean is. Pretend for a minute that all those trillions of gallons of water beneath you suddenly became solid ground. If you looked around, you'd see that not one place on that huge, huge area provides any shelter at all. There are no rocks, no trees, no caves— nothing to protect you from the sun or wind. Add to that the effects of cold water and waves, no easy access to fresh drinking water or food sources, and it's no wonder that surviving at sea is so challenging.

The ocean is one of the harshest environments on Earth, and humans are poorly designed to survive in it. We have no fins or gills like fish do to let us get our oxygen from the water. We don't have extra-capacity lungs or blowholes like whales, dolphins, or seals have to help them spend long periods of time underwater. Our bodies aren't sleek or **aerodynamic** like those of fish and sea mammals to make swimming underwater easy. We aren't covered in fur, and we don't have a thick, protective layer of blubber to keep us warm. We don't have wings or feathers like seabirds to allow us to fly above the waves and keep us insulated from sea spray.

Humans are built for land, not water. But even sea creatures are built for living *in* the water, not *on* it. In fact, if you are stuck adrift on the surface of the ocean, you're in an environment that no sea creature calls its permanent home. It's just too extreme.

Your body is pretty tough—you can last for weeks with no food and only a little water. You can tread water and float for hours, and even swim for miles if you have to, but if you can't find a way to keep your body protected from too much heat or too much cold, too much sun or too much wind, that tough body breaks down, quickly.

The Ocean's Sunscreen

Scientists have discovered that a chemical compound that can be found in lots of sea creatures makes a great natural sunscreen. It is called astaxanthin, and it is what makes krill, shrimp, salmon, and some sea algae red. Astaxanthin absorbs UV rays, which are the sun's rays that cause sunburn. When humans take astaxanthin, it can also reduce pain and swelling related to sunburn. Astaxanthin isn't a substitute for sunscreen—for one thing, you'd have to eat about three pounds of salmon a day to get enough astaxanthin to see any benefit at all—but scientists say that it is a great natural booster to regular sunscreen, and it's a tasty way to protect yourself!

SUN

One of the big challenges you face on the open ocean is protecting yourself from the effects of the sun. In tropical waters, the sun will be very intense because the closer you are to the equator, the more directly the sun's rays

hit the earth. The farther away you are from the equator, the less direct sunlight you'll receive. Depending on the season and where you are on the globe, you may have long days with lots of hot sun, or short days with very little sunlight.

Lots of direct sun usually means very warm air temperatures. With no trees or other objects for shade, your body has to work hard to keep cool. Your body can lose valuable water through sweating. If you can't find a way to cover yourself or replace those lost fluids, you can become dehydrated and overheat. In extreme situations, you could have heat exhaustion or heat stroke.

YOUR BODY DOESN'T LIKE EXTREMES

Most people have a normal body temperature somewhere between 97 and 99 degrees Fahrenheit (about 37 degrees Celsius)—it varies a bit from person to person. This temperature is a measure of your body's ability to make or get rid of heat. Your body systems work best at this temperature, and so your body automatically regulates itself to stay there, no matter what the surrounding air is like. On really hot days, for example, the air is warmer than your body temperature. You absorb some of this heat through your skin. Your body automatically responds to the extra heat by expanding the blood vessels in your skin to carry the excess heat away from your internal **organs** and out through your skin. Then your sweat glands produce sweat, which cools your skin as the sweat evaporates. It's like a built-in air conditioning unit; your body just does it for you.

WORDS TO KNOW

aerodynamic: having a shape that reduces the amount of drag when moving through the air or water, enabling an animal to move quickly through the air or water.

organ: a part of the body, such as the heart or lungs, that performs a certain function inside the body.

Your body can cope with some swings in temperature, but if your body can't keep its internal temperature within a few degrees of that ideal 97 to 99 range, bad things happen. When you are exposed to the sun all day long, you can be in danger from heat exhaustion or, more seriously, heat stroke.

Heat exhaustion and heat stroke happen when your body can't cool itself down. Heat exhaustion is when your body gets dehydrated and can't keep blood flowing both to your internal organs and to your skin to cool you down. So your body automatically sends the blood to the most important place: your vital organs. It sends less blood to your muscles and outer extremities. When that happens, your body temperature rises, your muscles cramp, and you may feel light-headed or sick to your stomach. The remedy for heat exhaustion is to move to a shaded area, loosen your clothing, and drink water, slowly, so you can replace those fluids and help your body systems get back to normal. But if you can't do these things, heat stroke is the next deadly result. Heat stroke happens because your body has no water left to cool itself. The result: your body temperature rises uncontrollably—in other words, you cook. You may lose consciousness. If you can't get help immediately, you'll die.

THE SUN CAN BURN YOU ANYTIME

The sun is also a problem in cold oceans—not because you can get dehydrated from sweating or get heat stroke, obviously—but because of the way water and sunlight interact. When the sun's rays hit the ocean surface, some of that light is absorbed into the water, which is how the surface of the ocean is warmed. But lots more of that light hits the water and is reflected back into the sky.

All that reflected light from the water hits you. And if enough reflected light hits you, you stand a really good chance of getting sunburned. It doesn't matter if you are in an ocean where the air temperature is 96 degrees Fahrenheit (35 degrees Celsius) or 32 degrees Fahrenheit (zero degrees Celsius); if the sun is shining, you can get sunburned. Sunburns are caused by **radiation**, not by heat. That's why you can get sunburned any time of the year, and even when there is snow on the ground. In fact, you can get sunburned even when the sky is cloudy. Water is such a good reflector of light, and the rays of the sun that can burn your skin are so good at traveling through cloud cover, that you should protect your skin even on the gloomiest-looking days.

WORDS TO KNOW

radiation: energy that is transmitted in the form of rays, waves, or particles from a source, such as the sun.

Sunburned Eyes

Did you know you can get sunburned eyes? It's often called "snow blindness" or "flash burn," but its official name is "photokeratitis." It happens when your corneas, the tissues on the surface of your eyes, get sunburned. Photokeratitis happens most frequently to skiers or mountain climbers who are on snow up high on sunny days, but it can definitely happen to you if you're on the ocean and the sun is bright.

The sun hits the water and reflects ultraviolet rays back up into the sky. If your eyes are unprotected, those rays also hit your eyes. If your eyes are exposed long enough, they'll get burned just like your skin burns. Symptoms of sunburned eyes are red, painful, or itchy eyes, hazy vision, or even a loss of vision altogether. Your eyes might feel like you have sand in them. But don't panic—just as most sunburns heal after a day or two, your sunburned eyes will also get better in about a day. Your corneas regenerate in one to two days, so your eyes should be just fine. But be sure to keep them closed as much as possible until they heal.

TRY THIS: MAKE A SUN-REFLECTOR MASK

You can make a simple sun shield that will help deflect some of the light that bounces off the water. You'll need a piece of cardboard, a pair of scissors, and a long rubber band cut so it is one long strip, or two pieces of string. Cut the cardboard into a mask the width of your face—make sure it covers the sides of your face, too. Cut two horizontal slits over your eyes—just enough to see out of. Poke holes in either side of the mask, and thread the rubber band through both sides. If you are using string, attach a piece of string to each hole. The mask should fit snugly enough on your face that the eye holes stay just over your eyes. You will be able to see enough to get by, but the ultraviolet rays bouncing off the water will also bounce off the cardboard and away from your eyes.

PROTECT YOURSELF WITH CLOTHES

You may have seen movies where the hero's boat is sinking, so he strips off his shirt and dives into the water to the life raft. That might sell movie tickets, but it's a bad idea in a real emergency. Your clothes are one of the most valuable forms of shelter at sea. Whether stuck in the tropics, where the sun is beating down from morning to night, or stranded in the northern oceans, where it's so cold that ice collects on the sides of your raft, you'll need clothes. Clothes are the first line of defense against both the heat and the cold. They'll protect you from the drying effects of the wind and the burning rays of the sun, and in cold places they will help you conserve your body heat.

In a hot climate, it is important to keep the top of your head and the back of your neck covered as much as possible. These are the most exposed parts of your body, and are often the first to burn. If you don't have a hat, use any other piece of clothing to make some kind of head and neck covering. If you have a choice of light or dark clothes, wear the lightest-colored clothes you can. Light-colored clothes reflect more light, and will keep you cooler.

In a cold climate, it's even more important to keep as many clothes on as possible. If your clothes are wet, take them off, squeeze out the water, and put them back on. Your clothes will dry faster without excess water in them and you'll warm up sooner without cold water next to your skin. If you have any extra clothes, take off your wet things one piece at a time (never take off all of your clothes at once—you want to keep as much of your skin covered as you can), and replace each one with something dry. If you have dark-colored clothes, wear them as the top layer because they will absorb more light and give you more heat.

If you've ever been outside on a hot day wearing a black shirt, you know that dark colors make you hotter than light ones. Why? Because dark colors absorb more of the sun's rays, and light colors reflect more. When white light (sunlight) hits something black, all of those light rays are absorbed and none are reflected. When white light hits something white, no light rays are absorbed and all are reflected. The darker the color, the more light rays are absorbed. That absorbed energy is transferred into heat energy. If you're wearing a black shirt, that heat energy is transferred to you, so you feel hotter!

Taking the Ocean's Temperature

In 2003, scientists launched the Argo Project, a worldwide project to measure the temperature and salinity (saltiness) of the surface layer of all the world's oceans. Scientists designed special instruments that are programmed to sink to 2,000 meters, and then measure the salinity and temperature of the water as they rise to the surface. These measurements help scientists monitor the changes in temperature and salinity that are occurring because of global warming. Right now more than 3,000 free-drifting floats are sending information about the top 2,000 meters of ocean to scientists all over the world.

TRY THIS: WHICH COLORS ABSORB MORE HEAT?

Here is a quick way to see light energy transferred to heat energy in action. Take two same-sized, clear glasses. Cover the outside of one with black paper and the other with tin foil, shiny side out. Fill both glasses with cold water from the faucet and put them in front of a heat source—it can be a small lamp or even a sunny window as long as both glasses are getting the same amount of light. Wait for an hour, and then take the temperature of each glass. Which glass has warmer water?

WATER TEMPERATURES AND YOUR BODY

The temperature of ocean water is dependent on two things: light and heat. You know that when the sun hits the surface of the ocean, some of its light and heat get absorbed by the surface layer of water. The currents, wind, and waves tumble that top layer pretty thoroughly, so the temperature of that surface layer is pretty much the same throughout. But the ocean temperature also depends where on Earth that ocean water is. The reason different parts of the

ocean have different surface temperatures is mostly because of latitude. The oceans that are closest to the equator have warm surface temperatures because they get the most direct sunlight, and the oceans that are farthest from the equator are the coldest because they get the least direct sunlight. That's why the temperature of the surface water in the polar oceans can be as cold as 28 degrees Fahrenheit (-2 degrees Celsius), and the temperature of the surface water in the Persian Gulf can be as warm as 96 degrees Fahrenheit (36 degrees Celsius).

But even in the warmest oceans, you can get really cold, especially if it's windy. In the worst case, you run the risk of **hypothermia**.

Hypothermia Is All About the "Umbles"

Because hypothermia is something that happens over time, you might not notice you have it until it's too late. These "umbles" are all signs of hypothermia:

Stumbles • Mumbles • Fumbles • Grumbles

WORDS TO KNOW

hypothermia: when the temperature inside your body is too cold.

When you get splashed with water and are cold, your body reacts automatically to the change in the air temperature surrounding it. The hair on your skin rises so it catches the slightly warmed air next to your body and holds it there to keep you in a little, warm, air bubble. The blood vessels in your skin contract (or tighten) so that less heat from your blood comes to your skin and is lost. If you're really cold, your body will make your muscles contract at the same time, making you shiver. That movement generates body heat. In really, really cold situations, your body will take blood away from the places farthest from your most vital organs such as your heart and lungs. That's why your fingers, nose, ears, and toes are the first to get cold and numb.

Hypothermia happens when your body temperature cools down so much that your internal organs can't keep warm enough. Hypothermia is sneaky: it affects your ability to think clearly and respond quickly to problems, and it affects your body more quickly than you realize— you don't have to be in super-cold temperatures to get it. All it takes for mild hypothermia to set in is sitting in wet clothes in a slight breeze, even on a warm day. The water in your clothes is chilled by the wind and air temperature, and your skin is chilled by the water. The blood vessels in your skin constrict to conserve heat, so you start to shiver to generate more. That shivering uses up valuable energy, which further stresses your body.

If you can't warm yourself from the outside, moderate hypothermia sets in. Your body systems start to shut down from the outside in: blood is routed away from your fingers, toes, feet, hands, and so on to conserve heat to your vital organs. You become really clumsy. You can't speak clearly. You can't think clearly. When you are dangerously hypothermic you stop shivering because you aren't generating enough warmth with your muscle contractions to benefit your body. The shivering automatically shuts down to save energy. If you get cold enough, your body goes into a hibernation mode, where your breathing and heart rate slow. If your body temperature goes below 85 degrees Fahrenheit (29 degrees Celsius), your heart rate becomes very erratic. You are unconscious. Your breathing is very shallow. If you can't start rewarming immediately, you will die.

Believe it or not, you can die from hypothermia in the tropical ocean, especially if you can't keep dry. Think about what happened to the crew of *Trashman*, a sailboat that was sunk by a 40-foot (12-meter) wave in a storm off the Florida coast. The crew members were left with a rubber dinghy and nothing else.

FASCINATING FACT

The average temperature of the surface water of all the world's oceans is about 62.6 degrees Fahrenheit (17 degrees Celsius).

Hypothermia and Water

You lose body heat 25 times faster in water than you do in the air. The colder the water, the faster you lose heat. Here's an estimate of how long most people can survive in different temperatures of water:

IF THE WATER TEMPERATURE (F) IS:	EXHAUSTION OR UNCONSCIOUSNESS	EXPECTED TIME OF SURVIVAL IS:
32.5	Under 15 minutes	Under 15 – 45 minutes
32.5 – 40.0	15 – 30 minutes	30 – 90 minutes
40.0 – 50.0	30 – 60 minutes	1 – 3 hours
50.0 – 60.0	1 – 2 hours	1 – 6 hours
60.0 – 70.0	2 – 7 hours	2 – 40 hours
70.0 – 80.0	3 – 12 hours	3 hours – indefinitely
OVER 80.0	Indefinitely	Indefinitely

For five days and nights they drifted in the stormy ocean with no food, water, or shelter. They had only the clothes they were wearing when their boat sank—shorts and T-shirts. Even though they were in warm water, the crew was exposed to wind and rain and quickly became hypothermic. They didn't have any way to dry their clothes, so to keep warm they took turns jumping over the side of the raft into the water, which was much warmer than the air. Each person stayed in the water for as long as they could hold on to the lifeline. Of the five crew members, only two survived—those two were the ones who could warm themselves in the water for the longest periods of time.

Insulation is a Mammal's Best Friend in Cold Water

What do sea mammals have that humans don't that allows them to live and thrive in the cold waters of the polar oceans? In a word, **blubber**. Whales, dolphins, porpoises, seals, sea lions, and walruses all have a thick layer of blubber beneath their skin that insulates them from the cold water of the ocean and allows them to maintain a constant body temperature. The blubber keeps the sea mammal warm by protecting it from cold, and is used as a source of energy to maintain body temperature. How much blubber each kind of creature has depends on the species. Arctic bowhead whales, for example, have blubber that is 20 inches (50 centimeters) thick to keep them warm in the super-cold Arctic seas. Seals and other **pinnipeds** can have blubber up to 3 inches (7.5 centimeters) thick.

Would people who have more fat on them have a better chance of surviving in the ocean than people with lower body fat? In theory, yes—their fat would act as insulation against the cold water and as a source of energy to help maintain a constant internal body temperature, very similar to sea mammals. But the difference between humans and sea mammals is that human bodies aren't designed to be covered in a heavy layer of fat. The heart, lungs, and internal organs of people who carry lots of excess fat on their bodies are already working harder than normal just to keep that body running properly. So while that extra fat would be useful to keep a person warm in the water, the extra weight would put lots of extra stress on their internal organs.

BLUBBER

TRY THIS: INSULATION

You don't have to jump into Arctic waters to see how much warmer you'd be with a nice thick coat of blubber. Try this experiment, instead. Fill two bowls with ice water. Coat one finger on one hand with petroleum jelly or vegetable shortening. Now stick the coated finger into one of the bowls of ice water and one finger on your other hand into the other bowl of ice water. Which finger gets colder faster?

YOU'RE A WATERY KID

You have a lot of water in you—in fact, water makes up 65 percent of your body. Your blood is mostly water, which makes sense, since blood is a liquid. But did you know that your organs, tissues, and joints all contain water, too? Your brain alone is about 80 percent water! Water plays a hugely important role in making your body work. It keeps your blood moving through your body, it lubricates your joints, and it keeps your muscles, nerves, and organs working together properly.

The water in your body isn't like the freshwater you drink. It contains electrolytes, which are a combination of minerals and salt. Electrolytes help your body's cells communicate effectively so that your muscles and nerves work properly. Without electrolytes, your body's cells just can't communicate properly—your muscles don't work right, your nerve cells don't make the right connections, and your organs have to work too hard and eventually shut down.

WORDS TO KNOW

blubber: an insulating layer of fat under the skin of whales and other large marine mammals.

pinniped: aquatic animals that use flippers to swim or move on land. The word means "wing-footed."

Babies Are Full of Water!

People have different percentages of water in their bodies depending on their age and sex. Babies have the most water in their bodies—they are almost 78 percent water. By the time babies turn one, their bodies are about 65 percent water. That's about how much water is in most kids' bodies throughout childhood. When kids become adults, the percentage of water in their body drops. Adult men are at about 60 percent water, and women are usually at 55 percent. Women have less water because they generally have more fat on their bodies than men do, and fat doesn't hold any water.

You lose electrolytes every day, through sweating, crying, and going to the bathroom. You replace those electrolytes through the foods you eat, and even through some of the liquids you drink. Your body automatically regulates the amount of electrolytes you have so that all your body systems work properly. Keeping the right balance of electrolytes isn't hard to do since your body does it all by itself, but the balance of electrolytes needs to stay the same or your body systems shut down.

If your body doesn't get enough water to replace the fluids you lose each day, you will become dehydrated. *Dehydration* simply means "lack of water." One of the most common problems you could face if stuck at sea would be becoming dehydrated—quickly. Being exposed to the sun all day means your body has to work hard to keep its temperature regulated, and so you sweat. When you sweat, you lose water and you lose electrolytes. If you can't replace those liquids, you become dehydrated. When you are dehydrated, your electrolyte levels get out of balance and your body systems don't work the way they should.

They have to work harder and harder to try to keep everything in balance, which stresses them even more. If you become very dehydrated, your body's systems become so overstressed that you can die.

Weirdly enough, the water in your body actually has just about the same combination of salts and minerals that seawater has. Since your body automatically keeps the amount of electrolytes balanced all by itself, and the water in your body and seawater have all the same kinds of minerals and salts, you'd think it would be no big deal to drink as much salt water as you wanted if you were thirsty, right? Wrong.

DON'T DRINK SEAWATER!

If you drink seawater, bad things happen. At the very least, you'll end up thirstier than you were before you drank it. If you drink a little too much, you'll get sick. Drink way too much and you'll die. Why? Because even though your body and seawater have the same minerals and salts, seawater has three times the quantity of them as your body does. Think about this: a cup of freshwater, the kind of water you like to drink and the kind your body needs, is about 0.05 percent salt. That's a really small amount. A cup of seawater is 3.5 percent salt. That's way, way more salt than your body needs—or can stand.

Your body automatically balances the amount of salts and minerals you have. When you drink seawater, you're pouring salt into your body. Your body goes on high alert, since all that salt will throw off your electrolyte balance. The water molecules in your cells rush to try and dilute the salt, pushing it out of the cells and into the bloodstream so it can be carried away. That leaves your cells without the right amount of water, so they get dehydrated—which means you do, too. Then all that salt that is now in your bloodstream goes into your kidneys, which have to work overtime to get that salt out of you. If you drink enough seawater, your kidneys will eventually get over-whelmed and shut down altogether.

— FASCINATING FACT —
Healthy adults have enough salt in their bodies to fill three saltshakers.

try this: Dehydration in action

Here is a great way to see how drinking seawater dehydrates your body. Find two bowls, some salt, and a potato. Fill two bowls with about a cup of cold water each. Mix about 2 tablespoons of salt into each of the bowls. Now cut two slices off the potato, each about 1/8 inch (25 millimeters) thick. Put one potato slice in each bowl. After 30 minutes, take the potato slices out of the water. The one in plain water will still be pretty crisp, if a little soggy. The slice that was in the salt water, though, will be so limp you can bend it in half. Why? Because the salt water in the bowl was saltier than the water in the potato. The freshwater in the potato was drawn to the salt water, leaving the potato and dehydrating its cells. If you were to measure the water in the saltwater bowl, there would be slightly more water in it than when you started. This is the same thing that would happen to your body's cells if you drank seawater.

You are better off drinking no water at all than drinking seawater. Think about what happened to the very unlucky crew of the *Columbian*, a ship that exploded and sank off the coast of Nova Scotia in 1914. Fifteen crew members made it off the sinking ship into a lifeboat. For two weeks the men drifted in the open ocean with almost no food and only one small cask of water. They rationed the water, and each crew member could drink only a tiny sip a couple of times each day. For some crew members, this just wasn't enough. They began to drink seawater, with disastrous results. One by one, the crew members lost their minds. The chief officer of the ship told his rescuers,

FASCINATING FACT

When seawater freezes into sea ice, the ice loses its salt content and turns into frozen freshwater. If you're in an area of the ocean with sea ice, you can suck on pieces of it for rehydration.

The Survival Rule of Three

Survival experts say that in general, people can live for three minutes with no air, three days with no water, three weeks with no food.

"The more they drank, the more they wanted. There was one tin dipper in the boat and I tried to keep it in my possession. But if I was asleep they would get it away from me . . . I would get the dipper away from the men who were swilling salt water, but the next minute they would be leaning out over the gunwale of the boat, lapping it up like cows at a brook. Soon they would go crazy. All of them died singing, completely insane." Of the fifteen men who survived the shipwreck, only four were rescued alive. None of the survivors had drunk seawater.

TRY THIS: DETERMINE HOW MUCH WATER YOU NEED PER DAY

While you probably won't ever be lost at sea and have to ration water (at least you'd better hope not!), it's important to know how much water you need to drink each day to stay healthy and fit. Most people say drinking eight 8-ounce glasses of water is the amount you need to stay hydrated, but that's just an average amount. You might need more or less, depending on your weight, where you live, your activity level, and what other liquids you drink. Here's a way to figure out exactly how much water *you* need. Find out how much you weigh in pounds. Divide that by two. That number equals the number of ounces of water your body needs each day to stay hydrated. To figure out about how many glasses of water that is, take the number of ounces you need and divide that by eight. That's about how many glasses of water you should drink on an average day. If you drink soda, sugared drinks, or drinks with caffeine, you need to add an extra glass of water. If you live in a hot or dry climate, add one more glass. And if you're an athlete and you exercise for more than half an hour, add another one. Is the total number of glasses of water you need more or less than you thought?

Warning!! Don't Drink Your Urine!

You may have seen survival experts on TV tell you that you can drink your urine if you're really desperate for water. Don't do it! Technically it's true that you can drink your own urine since it is about 95 percent water and is sterile (which means it doesn't have any bacteria in it). But like seawater, urine has a high salt content and can increase your chances of dehydration. If you have a **solar still**, you can distill the water from your urine just as you would seawater. But since your urine already contains all the stuff your kidneys have filtered out of your blood, you're really better off distilling seawater than recycling your pee.

WORDS TO KNOW

solar still: a way to distill water in which the power of the sun evaporates water, purifying it, and the purified water drips into a container.

convulsions: violent and uncontrollable muscle contractions.

Know the Symptoms of Dehydration

You don't have to be lost at sea to get dehydrated. If it's a hot day, or you're busy and forget to drink regularly, you can easily lose more water than you are taking in. Symptoms of mild dehydration include a dry mouth, flushed face, headache, dizziness, and dark urine. Your skin might be dry and you might start getting cramps in your muscles. You can usually fix mild dehydration by drinking water, one glass at a time, over the course of a couple of hours. People don't usually get severely dehydrated just by spending too much time outside. Instead, it is usually the result of being sick—throwing up and having diarrhea for a long time. If you're severely dehydrated, your blood pressure drops and you could go into **convulsions** or heart failure. Your skin loses its elasticity, so when you press your fingers into it, the skin doesn't bounce back and your fingerprints will stay. Other symptoms of severe dehydration include no tears, severe muscle contractions, and sunken eyes. Severe dehydration is life-threatening, and people who are severely dehydrated need medical attention right away.

WAYS TO FIND WATER IN THE OCEAN

So, if you are stranded at sea and don't have any freshwater, what do you do? There are a few different ways you can find drinking water at sea. You can collect water from rain, dew, or ice. You can distill water from seawater. And you can find water in creatures that live in the sea.

Collecting Rainwater

This is the simplest way to keep up a water supply. You can catch rainwater in any container, but it's most efficient to use a large piece of fabric, like a sail or plastic sheet.

You can see when a rain squall is coming—the clouds above you will be very gray, and you may even see a line of rain moving from the clouds to the waves. When you see a squall approach, rinse your rain-catching fabric in seawater. Why? You may not realize it, but everything around you is covered in salt crystals. As soon as that freshwater hits those salt crystals, it will turn salty. Rinsing off your water-catching fabrics in seawater will leave a little salt on them, it's true, but far less than if you were to leave all the dried salt crystals on the fabric.

Spread your rain-catching material so that it covers as much area as possible and shape it into a bowl so that rainwater will run into the middle and not out the sides.

Harvesting Dew

If there isn't any rain, you can still collect water from the air. When the sun goes down, the air cools. Cooler air holds less water vapor. That water vapor condenses into dew, which is fresh, drinkable water. Take your sail, tarp, or the largest piece of fabric you have and spread it out so that it covers as much area as possible. Turn up the corners so that when the water condenses it will roll toward the middle. You may not get much water each night, but you should get some, and that water can mean the difference between life and death.

TRY THIS: MAKE A SOLAR STILL

Another way to get freshwater is to make it. Believe it or not, you can actually create freshwater from seawater through a process called distillation. To distill something is to separate its chemical components. Using the heat of the sun, you can make a solar still that will separate the salt from seawater and gather the freshwater that is left. Solar stills aren't a very efficient way to get freshwater since the process takes a long time and you don't get very much water. But it's definitely better than no water at all.

All you need to make a simple solar still is a small container to hold seawater, a plastic bag that you can seal in some way, and some sun. Put the container of seawater inside the plastic bag, seal the bag (even tying a knot in the top will do), and put it in direct sunlight on as stable a surface as you can find.

The inside of the plastic bag will gradually heat up enough that the seawater will start to evaporate. Since the plastic bag is sealed, the water vapor can't escape. It rises to the top of the bag and begins to condense in freshwater droplets. These droplets will eventually run down the sides of the bag and collect in the bottom. The salt remains in the container. In the late evening or early morning you can unseal the plastic bag, carefully remove the saltwater container, then lick the freshwater from the inside of the plastic bag. It won't give you a lot of water at one time, but it doesn't take much energy to make. Any water is better than none at all.

HEAT

water vapor

plastic bag

container

sea water

fresh water

END NOTE

The Oceans Need Your Help!

Our oceans are in trouble and really need our help! Oceans absorb most of the carbon dioxide in the atmosphere, and return 70 percent of the oxygen we need to live on Earth. Scientists are warning us that our oceans are the key to keeping our climate cool and our planet healthy. We need to protect them before it's too late. Even though you're "just a kid," you can be a part of the solution to keep our oceans clean and healthy for generations of kids to come.

Eat lower on the food chain. Rather than eating large predators, such as tuna and swordfish, eat smaller fish that are much more plentiful in the ocean, such as anchovy or herrings. You wouldn't think about making a lion or tiger your favorite meal, would you? Think about ocean predators the same way.

Bring your own shopping bags to the store. Plastic is a major problem for our oceans. Plastic shopping bags by the thousands end up in the oceans, where sea turtles and other animals mistake them for jellyfish. When they eat the bags, the turtles die. Other plastics break down in the water and turn into a really toxic dust that coats undersea reefs. Fish eat from the reefs and the toxins end up in their flesh. We eat the fish, and so we are eating toxic dust, too. To learn where you can recycle plastic bags, go to www.earth911.org.

Green up your aquarium. Did you know that more than 90 percent of the tropical fish caught in the wild and sold to pet stores for saltwater aquariums end up dying, and the reefs they came from suffer, too? If you buy fish and plants for a saltwater aquarium, buy them from a store that raises their own. And when you clean or take apart a saltwater aquarium, don't let your fish and plants go back into the ocean! That's how invasive species are spread. A species of seaweed called *Caulerpa taxifolia* that was dropped into the Mediterranean Sea from someone who was cleaning out their saltwater aquarium is now completely smothering the waters there. And the lionfish, a poisonous fish from the tropical Pacific, is taking over the waters of the Bahamas after someone released a pet from their saltwater aquarium. Nonnative species don't have any natural predators, so they can easily overwhelm a new environment. Don't let that happen with your tank!

For more information about ocean conservation and how kids can help, check out some of these websites:

www.dolphinlog.org
www.earthforce.org
www.keepoceansclean.org
www.kidsforsavingearth.org
www.kidsplanet.org
www.oceanconservation.org
www.saveourseas.org

Get involved! Learn as much as you can about our oceans and how we can help keep them clean and healthy. There are lots of conservation organizations that love kids' help. Be a part of the solution— do something!

RESOURCES

Books

Bailey, Maurice and Maralyn. *Staying Alive!* New York: David McKay Company, 1974.

Ballard, Robert. *The Eternal Darkness: A Personal History of Deep-Sea Exploration.* Princeton, NJ: Princeton University Press, 2000.

Broad, Williams J. *The Universe Below: Discovering the Secrets of the Deep Sea.* New York: Simon & Schuster, 1997.

Ganeri, Anita. *The Oceans Atlas: A Pictorial Atlas of the World's Oceans.* London: Dorling Kindersley, 1994.

Gatty, Harold. *Finding Your Way Without Map or Compass.* Mineola, New York: Dover Publications, 1999.

Hall, Michele, and Hall, Ward. *Secrets of the Ocean ·Realm.* New York: Carol & Graf Publishers, 1997.

Hickman, Pamela. *Turtle Rescue.* Buffalo, New York: Firefly Books, 2005.

Hutchinson, Stephen, and Hawkins, Lawrence. *Oceans: A Visual Guide.* Buffalo, New York: Firefly Books, 2005.

Kiley, Deborah Scaling. *Albatross.* Boston: Houghton Mifflin Company, 1994.

Kunzig, Robert. *The Restless Sea: Exploring the World Beneath the Waves.* New York: W.W. Norton, 1999.

Kurlansky, Mark. *The Story of Salt.* New York: G.P. Putnam's Sons, 2006.

Leslie, Edward. *Desperate Journeys, Abandoned Souls: True Stories of Castaways and Other Survivors.* Boston: Houghton Mifflin Company, 1988.

Natural History of the Oceans. New York: DK Publishing, 2001.

O'Hanlon, Redmond. *Trawler.* New York: Knopf, 2005.

Robertson, Dougal. *Survive the Savage Sea.* New York: Praeger Publishers, 1973.

Sauvain, Philip. *Oceans.* Minneapolis, Minnesota: Carolrhoda Books, 1996.

Viera, Linda. *The Seven Seas.* New York: Walker & Company, 2003.

Magazine Articles

Black, Richard. "Protection needed for 'marine Serengitis.'" *BBC News,* April 8, 2004.

Young, Emma. "Polynesians Beat Columbus to Americas." *The New Scientist,* June 2, 2004.

"Biologists Close In on Mystery of Sea Turtles' 'Lost Years.'" *University of Florida,* October 3, 2007. Retrieved May 27, 2008, www.sciencedaily.com.

"Canteen Science: The Soggy Spud." *Odyssey Magazine,* February 2008, p. 26.

"Castaways Died Insane from Thirst." *The New York Times,* May 19, 1914.

"Dust Storms in Sahara Desert Trigger Huge Plankton Blooms in Eastern Atlantic." *National Oceanography Centre, University of Southampton,* February 10, 2008.

"Water from Thin Air—Harvesting Dew." *Odyssey Magazine,* February 2008, p. 27.

"World's Largest Marine Protected Area Created in Pacific Ocean." *Conservation International,* February 18, 2008.

GLOSSARY

abyssopelagic zone: the ocean zone that stretches from a depth of 13,124 to 19,686 feet.

adaptation: changes an animal or plant makes (or has made) in response to its environment.

aerodynamic: having a shape that reduces the amount of drag when moving through the air or water, enabling an animal to move quickly through the air or water.

algae: a plant-like organism that turns light into energy, but that does not have leaves or roots.

antidote: medicine that stops the effects of poison.

apex: the top point.

atmosphere: the layer of air surrounding the earth.

axis: the center, around which something rotates.

basin: a natural depression in the surface of land or underwater.

bathypelagic zone: the zone of the ocean that stretches from a depth of 3,281 and 13,124 feet.

bioluminescence: the ability to create light from a chemical reaction inside an organism's body.

biosphere: the part of the earth's crust, waters, and atmosphere that supports life.

bleaching: when coral dies, it loses its color and becomes white, or bleached.

blubber: an insulating layer of fat under the skin of whales and other large marine mammals.

cannibalism: eating a human being.

canyon: a deep trench in the earth, often with steep sides.

cell: the most basic unit of all organisms. Billions of cells make up an animal or plant.

census: a gathering of data.

chemosynthesis: a process through which organisms get energy from carbon dioxide and water instead of sun.

chronometer: an accurate clock used in navigation.

climate: the prevailing weather conditions of a region—temperature, air pressure, humidity, precipitation, sunshine, cloudiness, and winds—throughout the year, averaged over a series of years.

constellation: a group of stars in the sky that resembles a certain shape, such as the Big Dipper.

continental plates: the different portions of the earth's crust that move over a long time.

convulsions: violent and uncontrollable muscle contractions.

copepod: a tiny animal related to shrimp.

current: a steady flow of water in a certain direction.

degree: a unit of measurement that tells people where they are on the planet.

dehydrated: when you haven't had enough water and your body needs it.

desalination: the process of removing salt from water.

distillation: the process of making a liquid such as ocean water safe for drinking by boiling it and collecting the water vapor.

ecosystem: a community of plants and animals relying on each other to survive.

Endangered Species Act: an act passed by Congress to protect plants and animals from extinction.

equator: the imaginary line around the earth, midway between the North and South Poles.

GLOSSARY

erosion: the process through which the earth is broken down and washed away by wind and water.

flying fish: a type of fish that has large, winglike fins that allow it to jump out of the water and glide for a short time.

food chain: a community of animals and plants where each different plant or animal is eaten by another plant or animal higher up in the chain.

global warming: an increase in the average temperature of the earth's atmosphere, causing climate change.

habitat: the environment or place where an organism or group of organisms lives.

hadalpelagic zone: the trench zone of the ocean, beginning at a depth of 19,686 feet and going all the way to the bottom of the ocean.

horizon: the point in the distance where the sky and the earth seem to meet.

hydrostatic pressure: the measure of the pressure at a given depth underwater.

hypothermia: when the temperature inside your body is too cold.

ice worms: a species of worm that lives in ice.

ichthyologist: a scientist who studies fish.

landlocked: surrounded by land.

larvae: the young form of a species that usually looks like a grub, such as a tadpole.

latitude: an imaginary line that goes around the earth and runs parallel to the equator. It measures your position on earth north or south of the equator.

longitude: imaginary lines running through the North and South Poles that indicate where you are on the globe.

Mariana Trench: the deepest part of the world's oceans, located in the Pacific, near Guam.

methane: a colorless, odorless gas that we use as a fuel.

midnight zone: the part of the ocean with no light.

molecules: the simplest part of an element (like oxygen) or a compound (like water).

monsoon: the rainy season. A time of year when it rains frequently in a certain part of the world.

nautical mile: a measurement of distance used on the ocean (6,082 feet or 1,853 meters) that is longer than a regular land mile.

Northern Hemisphere: the half of the globe, north of the equator.

nutrients: a source of nourishment for animals and plants, found in food.

ocean floor: the very bottom of the ocean.

oceanographer: a scientist who studies the ocean.

organ: a part of the body, such as the heart or lungs, that performs a certain function inside the body.

osmosis: the process of moving water through a filter that can make it good for drinking.

Persian Gulf: a part of the Indian Ocean, located in the Middle East.

Phoenicians: a civilization located on the shores of North Africa and the eastern Mediterranean Sea around the year 1000 BCE.

GLOSSARY

photosynthesis: the process through which organisms get energy from the sun.

phytoplankton: a type of plankton that gets its energy from the sun through photosynthesis.

pinniped: aquatic animals that use flippers to swim or move on land. The word means "wing-footed."

plankton: microscopic plants and animals that float or drift in great numbers in bodies of water.

polar ice cap: giant sheets of sea ice that float on the Arctic and Antarctic Oceans.

polyps: small creatures that live in colonies and form coral.

predator: an animal that lives by preying on, or eating, other animals.

pressure: the force that pushes upon any object.

prey: an animal that is hunted or caught for food.

protein: a compound found in many foods such as meat and eggs that we and other animals need to survive.

radiation: energy transmitted in the form of rays, waves, or particles from a source, such as the sun.

ration: an amount of food or water allowed per day in order to make the food or water last as long as possible.

Red Sea: a sea located between Africa and Saudi Arabia.

Sahara Desert: the largest desert in the world, located in northern Africa.

Sargasso Sea: an area in the North Atlantic that is surrounded by currents but that has no currents of its own. It is full of seaweed and has very few living animals.

seafloor: the bottom of the sea or ocean.

sea ice: ocean water that freezes.

sea mount: a mountain rising above the sea floor.

sediment: dirt, fertilizer, rocks, and other pieces of matter deposited in a river and in the ocean.

solar still: a way to distill water in which the power of the sun evaporates water, purifying it, and the purified water drips into a container.

sonar: an instrument that locates objects with sound waves.

sounding: measuring the depth of water.

Southern Hemisphere: the half of the globe south of the equator.

species: a group of living things that are closely related and physically similar.

submarine: a type of ship that travels beneath the water rather than above it and that can stay underwater for a long time.

sunlight zone: the top layer of the ocean.

swim bladder: an air-filled sac in many fish that helps them float.

temperate: the climate in the temperate zone, the regions north and south of the tropics.

thermohaline: a type of current that moves vast amounts of water around the world.

tropical: the climate in the tropics, the region north and south of the equator.

twilight zone: the layer below the sunlight zone that has no light at its bottom.

venom: poison given off by some animals and insects.

zooplankton: tiny ocean animals, like some jellyfish.

90

Index

Index